D1384473

Southern Living
what's for
supper

30-Minute Meals Everyone
Will Love

Oxmoor
HOUSE®

©2012 by Time Home Entertainment Inc.
135 West 50th Street, New York, NY 10020

Southern Living® is a registered trademark of Time Inc. Lifestyle Group. All rights reserved. No part of this book may be reproduced in any form or by any means without the prior written permission of the publisher, excepting brief quotations in connection with reviews written specifically for inclusion in magazines or newspapers, or limited excerpts strictly for personal use.

Hardcover
ISBN-13: 978-0-8487-3651-4
ISBN-10: 0-8487-3651-6

Softcover
ISBN-13: 978-0-8487-3642-2
ISBN-10: 0-8487-3642-7

Printed in the United States of America
First Printing 2012

Oxmoor House
VP, Publishing Director: Jim Childs
Senior Brand Manager: Daniel Fagan
Senior Editor: Rebecca Brennan
Managing Editor: Rebecca Benton

Southern Living® What's for Supper
Editor: Susan Hernandez Ray
Project Editor: Holly D. Smith
Senior Designer: Melissa Clark
Director, Test Kitchen: Elizabeth Tyler Austin
Assistant Directors, Test Kitchen:
   Julie Christopher, Julie Gunter
Test Kitchen Professionals: Wendy Ball, R.D.;
   Allison E. Cox; Victoria E. Cox; Margaret Monroe Dickey;
   Alyson Moreland Haynes; Stefanie Maloney; Callie Nash;
   Catherine Crowell Steele; Leah Van Deren
Photography Director: Jim Bathie
Senior Photo Stylist: Kay E. Clarke
Associate Photo Stylist: Katherine Eckert Coyne
Assistant Photo Stylist: Mary Louise Menendez
Senior Production Manager: Greg A. Amason

Contributors
Editor: Vanessa McNeil Rocchio
Copy Editor: Dawn Cannon
Proofreaders: Donna Baldone, Adrienne Davis,
   Barry Wise Smith
Test Kitchen Professionals: Tamara Goldis, Erica Hopper,
   Kathleen Royal Phillips, Lindsay A. Rozier
Photographer: Becky Luigart-Stayner
Interns: Laura Hoxworth, Alison Loughman, Anna Pollock

Southern Living®
Editor: M. Lindsay Bierman
Executive Editors: Rachel Hardage, Jessica S. Thuston
Food Director: Shannon Sliter Satterwhite
Test Kitchen Director: Rebecca Kracke Gordon
Senior Writer: Donna Florio
Senior Food Editors: Shirley Harrington, Mary Allen Perry
Recipe Editor: JoAnn Weatherly
Assistant Recipe Editor: Ashley Arthur
Test Kitchen Professionals: Norman King, Pam Lolley,
   Angela Sellers
Senior Photographers: Ralph Anderson, Gary Clark,
   Art Meripol
Photographers: Robbie Caponetto, Laurey W. Glenn
Photo Research Coordinator: Ginny P. Allen
Senior Photo Stylist: Buffy Hargett
Editorial Assistant: Pat York

Time Home Entertainment Inc.
Publisher: Richard Fraiman
VP, Strategy & Business Development: Steven Sandonato
Executive Director, Marketing Services: Carol Pittard
Executive Director, Retail & Special Sales: Tom Mifsud
Executive Director, New Product Development:
   Peter Harper
Director, Bookazine Development & Marketing:
   Laura Adam
Publishing Director: Joy Butts
Finance Director: Glenn Buonocore
Assistant General Counsel: Helen Wan

To order additional publications, call 1-800-765-6400 or 1-800-491-0551.

For more books to enrich your life,
visit **oxmoorhouse.com**

To search, savor, and share thousands
of recipes, visit **myrecipes.com**

Cover: Tomato-and-Corn Pizza (page 206)
Back cover: Lemon Chicken, Oregano Green Beans
   (page 43)
Page 1: Okra-and-Corn Maque Choux (page 73)

contents

welcome

As a busy working mom, I'm familiar with the daunting challenge of getting delicious, family-pleasing meals to the table on hectic weeknights. "What's for supper?" is the all-too-common question, and we're all looking for simple solutions that fit into our fast-paced schedules. I'll help you solve your dinnertime dilemmas with some quick-and-easy recipes and insightful tips that I've learned over the years, starting with cooking in the kitchen at a young age after my mother wouldn't let me have an Easy-Bake oven and continuing through the past twenty-two years of working in the *Southern Living* Test Kitchen.

In *Dinner's in the Pantry,* you'll find ways to skip the shopping and create delicious meals from staples like dried pasta, rice, and canned beans and vegetables. Other chapters include quick suppers to help you avoid the drive-through, no-cook suppers that can be whipped up without even turning on the oven, and slow-cooker meals that can be ready when you walk in the door. Find recipes that everyone will like in the *Picky Eaters* chapter and look for perfectly portioned recipes in *Cooking for Two.* There's even a *Weeknight Company* chapter full of recipes sure to impress your dinner guests without hours of stressful preparation. And, best of all, the recipes in this collection require no more than thirty minutes of prep.

Throughout the book you'll notice *Vanessa's Savvy Secrets,* where I share test kitchen secrets and technique tips; *Sidekicks,* convenient side-dish suggestions; and insider *Time-Saving Tips.* I've even included *Table Talk*—dinnertime conversation starters to help your family connect at the table.

So don't stress the next time your family asks, "What's for supper?" You'll be prepared with quick-and-easy test kitchen-approved recipes for every occasion. Even in the hustle and bustle of weeknight chaos, gather 'round the table, and enjoy supper together.

Vanessa McNeil Rocchio

Vanessa McNeil Rocchio
Test Kitchen Specialist/Food Styling

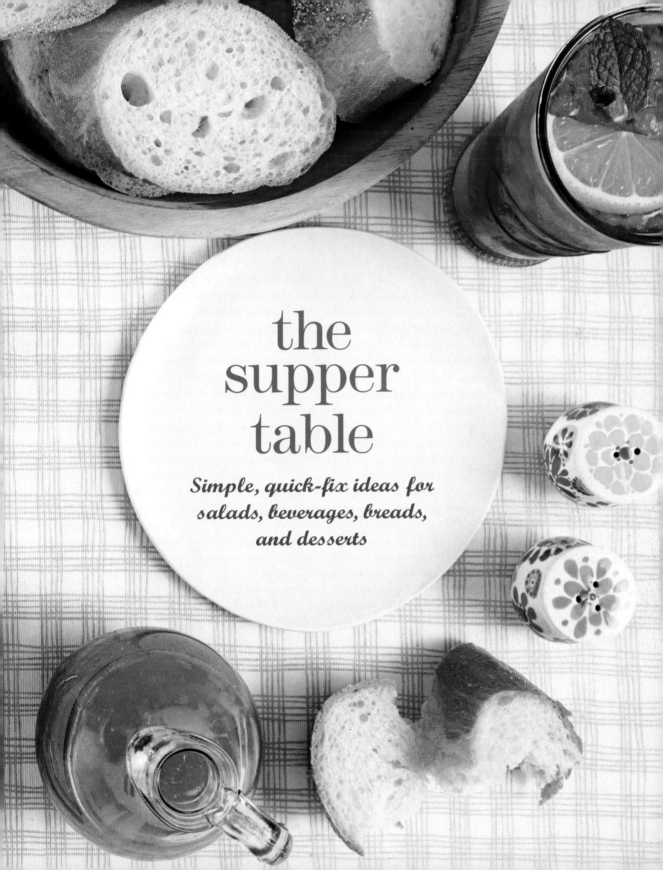

the supper table

*Simple, quick-fix ideas for
salads, beverages, breads,
and desserts*

Salads are fun and like a painting...

Select items from several of these groupings to build a tasty side dish.

fresh fruits:

sliced peaches   blackberries   strawberries

fresh herbs:

oregano   mint   thyme   basil

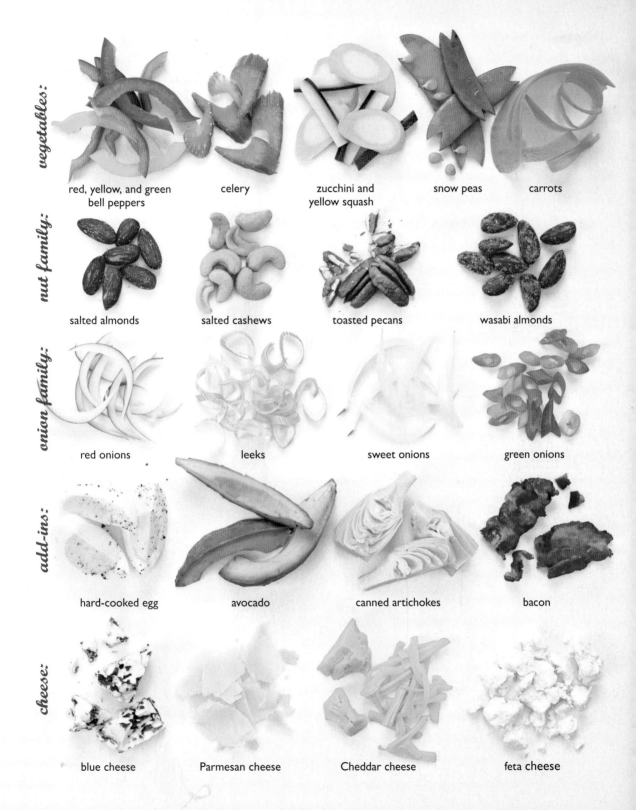

vegetables:

red, yellow, and green
bell peppers

celery

zucchini and
yellow squash

snow peas

carrots

nut family:

salted almonds

salted cashews

toasted pecans

wasabi almonds

onion family:

red onions

leeks

sweet onions

green onions

add-ins:

hard-cooked egg

avocado

canned artichokes

bacon

cheese:

blue cheese

Parmesan cheese

Cheddar cheese

feta cheese

Tea goes with just about anything in the South.

for company
Southern Sweet Tea

MAKES 2½ QT.
HANDS-ON TIME: 5 MIN.   **TOTAL TIME: 21 MIN.**

3	cups water	½	to 1 cup sugar
2	family-size tea bags	7	cups cold water

1. Bring 3 cups water to a boil in a saucepan; add tea bags. Boil 1 minute; remove from heat. Cover and steep 10 minutes.

2. Remove and discard tea bags. Add desired amount of sugar, stirring until dissolved. Pour into a 1-gal. container, and add 7 cups cold water. Serve over ice.

Peach Iced Tea: Prepare Southern Sweet Tea using ½ cup sugar. Stir together 1½ qt. tea, 1 (46-oz.) bottle peach nectar, and 2 Tbsp. lemon juice. Serve over ice. Makes 3 qt.

tea bags:

raspberry blueberry orange cinnamon

fruits:

lemon lime kiwi frozen grapes

juices:

pomegranate lemonade orange limeade

herbs & spices:

crystallized ginger mint cinnamon sticks basil

extras:

grenadine almond extract sugar cubes molasses

Beyond bread and butter...

Add some flavor to your
fresh-from-the-oven favorites.

baguette of
French bread

fresh herbs:

parsley   rosemary   oregano   basil

butter add-ins:

garlic   chive   roasted red repper   onion

dried herbs:

lemon pepper   Italian seasoning   Creole seasoning   dried crushed
                                                               red pepper

cheese:

goat   Parmesan   garlic-herb cheese   Cheddar

extras:

olive oil   flavored oil   chili oil   herbed oil

How far can a scoop of ice cream go?

chocolate sauce

refrigerated
whipped cream

sprinkles

strawberry sauce

chewy candies

chocolate morsels

crushed cookies

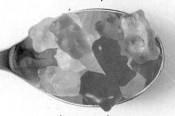

bananas

marshmallows

cherries

dinner's in the pantry

Pull together boxes of pasta, cans of vegetables, bags of rice, and other ingredients for a tasty meal

Skillet Lasagna

MAKES 6 SERVINGS
HANDS-ON TIME: 28 MIN.   TOTAL TIME: 38 MIN.

1	small onion, chopped	¼	tsp. salt
1	tsp. minced garlic	¼	tsp. dried crushed red pepper
1	Tbsp. olive oil	½	cup low-fat ricotta cheese
1	(24-oz.) jar tomato-and-basil pasta sauce	1	cup (4 oz.) shredded Italian six-cheese blend
½	(12-oz.) package multigrain extra-wide egg noodles	2	Tbsp. chopped fresh basil (optional)

1. Sauté onion and garlic in hot oil in a 10-inch skillet over medium heat 5 minutes or until onion is tender. Stir in pasta sauce, egg noodles, and 1 cup water. Bring to a boil; reduce heat to medium low, and simmer, stirring occasionally, 8 to 10 minutes or until pasta is just tender and liquid is almost absorbed. Stir in salt and crushed red pepper.

2. Stir together ricotta and ½ cup shredded cheese. Drop by heaping tablespoonfuls over pasta. Sprinkle with remaining ½ cup cheese.

3. Cook, covered, over low heat 5 minutes or until thoroughly heated and cheese is melted. Remove from heat, and let stand 5 minutes. Sprinkle with basil, if desired.

Note: We tested with Classico Tomato & Basil pasta sauce.

flavor profile: fresh basil

This tasty herb has a clean, bright flavor with hints of licorice and cloves.

sidekick: **SPINACH-PARMESAN SALAD** Toss together 1 (10-oz.) package fresh spinach; 1 medium-size red onion, thinly sliced; 2 hard-cooked eggs, chopped; 1 cup garlic-seasoned croutons; and 2 Tbsp. grated Parmesan cheese. Serve with bottled dressing.

Mexican Beef 'n' Rice

MAKES 6 SERVINGS
HANDS-ON TIME: 16 MIN.   **TOTAL TIME: 41 MIN.**

1½ lb. lean ground beef
½ cup chopped onion
1 (15.5-oz.) can black beans, drained and rinsed
1 cup refrigerated salsa
2 Tbsp. chopped fresh cilantro
1 Tbsp. fresh lime juice

1 (8.5-oz.) pouch ready-to-serve whole-grain Santa Fe rice
Toppings: chopped fresh cilantro, salsa, guacamole, shredded Cheddar cheese, fresh lime juice

1. Cook ground beef and onion in a large skillet over medium-high heat, stirring often, 6 to 8 minutes or until meat crumbles and is no longer pink; drain. Wipe skillet clean.

2. Combine ground beef mixture, beans, and next 3 ingredients in skillet, and cook 3 to 4 minutes or until thoroughly heated.

3. Prepare Santa Fe rice according to package directions. Stir in beef mixture. Serve with desired toppings.

Note: We tested with Uncle Ben's Ready Whole Grain Medley Santa Fe Rice.

sidekick: **SOUTHWESTERN CORNBREAD** Prepare 1 (19-oz.) package white cornbread mix according to package directions, stirring 1 cup (4 oz.) freshly shredded Monterey Jack cheese and 1 jalapeño pepper, seeded and finely chopped, into batter.

kid favorite

Cumin-Crusted Pork Cutlets

MAKES 4 TO 6 SERVINGS
HANDS-ON TIME: 27 MIN.   **TOTAL TIME: 27 MIN.**

3	whole wheat bread slices	½	tsp. salt
2	Tbsp. self-rising yellow cornmeal mix	¼	tsp. pepper
½	tsp. ground cumin	I	large egg
8	thinly sliced boneless pork loin chops (about 1¼ lb.)	2	Tbsp. whole grain mustard
		¼	cup olive oil

1. Process bread in a food processor until finely crumbled. Combine breadcrumbs, cornmeal mix, and cumin in a shallow bowl.

2. Sprinkle pork chops with salt and pepper. Whisk together egg, mustard, and 2 Tbsp. water until blended. Dip pork in egg mixture; dredge in breadcrumb mixture, pressing to adhere.

3. Cook half of pork in 2 Tbsp. hot oil in a large nonstick skillet over medium heat 3 to 4 minutes on each side or until golden brown. Keep warm in a 200° oven. Repeat procedure with remaining pork and oil. Serve warm.

sidekick: **CABBAGE-AND-APPLE SLAW** Sauté 4 cups shredded red cabbage, I cup thinly sliced sweet onion, and I thinly sliced Granny Smith apple in 2 Tbsp. hot olive oil until tender. Add 2 Tbsp. each red wine vinegar and brown sugar, and cook until sugar is dissolved. Sprinkle with salt and pepper to taste.

Easy Lasagna

MAKES 6 TO 8 SERVINGS
HANDS-ON TIME: 20 MIN.   TOTAL TIME: 1 HR., 30 MIN.

1	(1-lb.) package mild Italian sausage, casings removed	2	(24-oz.) jars tomato-and-basil pasta sauce
1	(15-oz.) container low-fat ricotta cheese	9	no-boil lasagna noodles
¼	cup jarred refrigerated pesto	4	cups (16 oz.) shredded Italian three-cheese blend or mozzarella cheese
1	large egg, lightly beaten		

1. Preheat oven to 350°. Lightly grease a 13- x 9-inch baking dish. Cook sausage in a large skillet over medium heat, stirring often, 8 to 10 minutes or until meat crumbles and is no longer pink; drain sausage well on paper towels.

2. Stir together ricotta cheese, pesto, and egg.

3. Spread half of 1 jar pasta sauce into prepared baking dish. Layer with 3 lasagna noodles (noodles should not touch each other or sides of dish), half of ricotta mixture, half of sausage, 1 cup three-cheese blend, and remaining half of 1 jar pasta sauce. Repeat layers using 3 lasagna noodles, remaining ricotta mixture, remaining sausage, and 1 cup three-cheese blend. Top with remaining 3 noodles and second jar of pasta sauce, covering noodles completely. Sprinkle with remaining 2 cups three-cheese blend.

4. Bake, covered, at 350° for 40 minutes. Uncover and bake 15 more minutes or until cheese is melted and edges are lightly browned and bubbly. Let stand 15 minutes.

Note: We tested with Classico Tomato & Basil pasta sauce.

flavor profile: refrigerated pesto

This Italian favorite can be used as a spread for meats or breads or it can be mixed in dishes. Pour any excess oil from top of pesto, and discard; then measure the pesto.

sidekick: **GARLIC BREAD**

Preheat oven to 350°. Stir together 3 garlic cloves, minced; 2 Tbsp. extra virgin olive oil; 2 Tbsp. butter, melted; 1 Tbsp. chopped fresh chives; and ½ tsp. dried crushed red pepper in a small bowl. Cut 1 (16-oz.) French bread loaf in half lengthwise. Brush cut sides with garlic mixture; place on a baking sheet. Bake at 350° for 13 to 15 minutes or until golden brown. Cut each bread half into 8 slices.

Spaghetti with Sausage and Peppers

MAKES 4 SERVINGS
HANDS-ON TIME: 30 MIN.   TOTAL TIME: 30 MIN.

8	oz. uncooked spaghetti	2 to 3	garlic cloves, minced
1	(1-lb.) package mild Italian	1	Tbsp. olive oil
	sausage, casings removed	1	(28-oz.) can diced tomatoes
1	medium onion, cut into		with basil, garlic, and
	eighths		oregano
1	medium-size green bell	¼	tsp. salt
	pepper, cut into strips	¼	tsp. pepper
1	medium-size red or yellow	½	cup grated Parmesan cheese
	bell pepper, cut into strips		Garnish: Parmesan cheese

1. Prepare pasta according to package directions.

2. Meanwhile, cook sausage in a large Dutch oven over medium-high heat, stirring often, 8 to 10 minutes or until meat crumbles and is no longer pink. Drain sausage well on paper towels; discard drippings.

3. Sauté onion and next 3 ingredients in hot oil in Dutch oven over medium-high heat 5 to 6 minutes or until vegetables are crisp-tender. Stir in tomatoes, salt, and pepper; cook 4 minutes or until thoroughly heated. Stir in sausage, pasta, and cheese. Transfer mixture to serving platter, and garnish, if desired. Serve immediately.

To freeze: Prepare recipe as directed. Cool 30 minutes. Place pasta mixture in a 13- x 9-inch baking dish. Cover tightly with plastic wrap and aluminum foil. Freeze up to 2 months. Thaw in refrigerator 24 hours. Preheat oven to 350°. Remove and discard plastic wrap. Cover with aluminum foil, and bake at 350° for 40 to 45 minutes or until thoroughly heated.

savvy secret
from Vanessa:

Fresh Italian sausage adds a nice twist to a dish typically made with ground beef. It adds extra flavor to recipes, and you can find it in the meat case at your super-market. To remove casings, cut through casing lengthwise on one side of each sausage. Remove meat, discard casings, and place meat in a large nonstick skillet or Dutch oven.

Jambalaya

MAKES 6 SERVINGS
HANDS-ON TIME: 30 MIN.   **TOTAL TIME: 55 MIN.**

1	lb. andouille sausage, cut into ¼-inch-thick slices	2	Tbsp. chopped fresh parsley
1	(10-oz.) package frozen vegetable seasoning blend	1	tsp. Cajun seasoning
1	(32-oz.) container low-sodium chicken broth	2	tsp. Worcestershire sauce
1	(14.5-oz.) can diced fire-roasted tomatoes with garlic	⅛	tsp. ground red pepper (optional)
2	cups uncooked long-grain rice	2	Tbsp. thinly sliced green onions

1. Cook sausage in a large Dutch oven over medium-high heat, stirring often, 8 to 10 minutes or until browned. Remove sausage with a slotted spoon, reserving drippings in Dutch oven; drain sausage on paper towels.

2. Add vegetable seasoning blend to hot drippings in Dutch oven, and sauté 3 to 5 minutes or until thoroughly heated. Add broth, next 5 ingredients, sausage, and, if desired, ground red pepper. Bring to a boil; cover, reduce heat to low, and simmer 18 to 20 minutes or until rice is tender and liquid is absorbed. Top with green onions, and serve immediately.

Note: We tested with McKenzie's Seasoning Blend frozen vegetables and Hunt's Fire Roasted Tomatoes Diced With Garlic.

time-saving tip: Diagonally sliced green onions make an eye-catching topping. To quickly slice them diagonally, hold the knife at a 45-degree angle to the green onions and slice them to desired thickness.

table talk: Bring Mardi Gras to the kitchen any time of year—this traditional Creole dish provides the perfect opportunity to decorate the table with carnival beads and masks. Let everyone choose their favorite beads and masks to wear for a festive, celebratory dinner.

kid favorite

Cooktop Cassoulet

MAKES 8 SERVINGS
HANDS-ON TIME: 28 MIN.   TOTAL TIME: 48 MIN.

1 lb. smoked sausage, cut into ½-inch rounds	1 (14.5-oz.) can diced tomatoes
4 skinned and boned chicken breasts, diced (about 1½ lb.)	1 bay leaf
1 large onion, chopped (about 1½ cups)	1 tsp. dried thyme
1 green bell pepper, chopped (about 1 cup)	¼ tsp. salt
1 garlic clove, minced	¼ tsp. pepper
	2 (16-oz.) cans great Northern beans
	¼ cup chicken broth

1. Cook sausage in a large skillet over medium-high heat, stirring often, 10 minutes or until browned. Remove sausage with a slotted spoon, and drain on paper towels; reserve drippings in skillet.

2. Sauté chicken in reserved drippings in skillet 8 to 10 minutes or until done; remove chicken with slotted spoon, and drain on paper towels. Reserve drippings in skillet.

3. Sauté onion, bell pepper, and garlic in reserved hot drippings in skillet 5 to 6 minutes or until tender. Stir in chicken, sausage, tomatoes, and next 4 ingredients. Bring to a boil, stirring occasionally; cover, reduce heat to low, and simmer 10 minutes. Stir in beans and broth. Cook, covered, 10 more minutes. Remove and discard bay leaf.

sidekick: **CORN MUFFINS** Preheat oven to 400°. Lightly grease a 24-cup miniature muffin pan. Stir together 1 (6.5-oz.) package corn muffin mix, ⅓ cup fat-free milk, 2 Tbsp. canola oil, 2 egg whites, and 1 cup frozen white shoepeg corn in a medium bowl just until blended. Spoon batter into prepared muffin pan. Bake 11 minutes. Spray tops of muffins with cooking spray; bake 2 more minutes. Remove from oven; cool in pan 2 minutes.

healthy

Spicy Pork-and-Orange Chopped Salad

MAKES 4 SERVINGS
HANDS-ON TIME: 28 MIN.   TOTAL TIME: 33 MIN.

1 lb. pork tenderloin, cut into ½-inch pieces	1 cup seeded and chopped cucumber
2 tsp. Chinese five spice	¼ cup chopped fresh cilantro
½ tsp. salt	1 romaine lettuce heart, chopped
¼ tsp. ground red pepper	3 cups shredded coleslaw mix
1 Tbsp. olive oil	½ cup wasabi-and-soy sauce-flavored almonds
2 oranges	Garnish: orange slices
½ cup bottled low-fat sesame-ginger dressing	

1. Toss pork with next 3 ingredients to coat. Sauté pork in hot oil in a large nonstick skillet over medium-high heat 6 minutes or until done.

2. Peel oranges, and cut into ½-inch-thick slices. Cut slices into bite-size chunks.

3. Pour dressing into a salad bowl. Stir in orange slices, cucumber, and cilantro. Let stand 5 minutes. Add romaine, coleslaw mix, and pork; toss gently. Sprinkle with almonds. Garnish, if desired. Serve immediately.

Note: We tested with Blue Diamond Bold Wasabi & Soy Sauce Almonds.

flavor profile: wasabi-and-soy sauce-flavored almonds

These nuts add a nice crunch to the salad and are a new favorite in our Test Kitchen. Find them sold in cans alongside cocktail peanuts.

Chicken Thigh Cacciatore

MAKES 4 SERVINGS
HANDS-ON TIME: 28 MIN.   **TOTAL TIME: 33 MIN.**

8	skinned and boned chicken thighs (about 2 lb.)
2	tsp. dried Italian seasoning
1	tsp. salt
2	Tbsp. vegetable oil
1	small onion, chopped
1	medium-size green bell pepper, chopped
1	garlic clove, minced
1	(24-oz.) jar tomato-and-basil pasta sauce
	Hot cooked fettuccine
⅓	cup chopped fresh parsley (optional)

1. Sprinkle chicken with Italian seasoning and salt. Cook chicken in hot oil in a 12-inch skillet over medium-high heat 5 to 6 minutes on each side or until done. Remove chicken; reserve drippings in skillet.

2. Sauté onion and bell pepper in hot drippings 4 minutes. Add garlic, and sauté 1 minute. Return chicken to skillet; pour pasta sauce over chicken. Bring to a boil over medium heat. Reduce heat to medium low, and simmer 3 to 5 minutes or until thoroughly heated.

3. Spoon chicken mixture over hot cooked fettuccine. Sprinkle with parsley, if desired.

sidekick: **BROCCOLI WITH GARLIC** Microwave 1 (12-oz.) package fresh broccoli florets; 1 garlic clove, minced; 2 Tbsp. water; and ½ tsp. salt in a microwave-safe glass bowl, covered with plastic wrap, at HIGH 3 to 4 minutes or until tender.

time-saving tip:

Purchase prechopped onion from the produce section of the grocery store rather than chopping your own. One small onion equals about ¾ cup chopped.

kid favorite

Chicken Thighs with Chunky Tomato Sauce 'n' Potatoes

MAKES 4 TO 6 SERVINGS
HANDS-ON TIME: 30 MIN. **TOTAL TIME: 33 MIN.**

1	(24-oz.) package frozen steam-and-mash potatoes	1	(14.5-oz.) can diced fire-roasted tomatoes with garlic
2	lb. skinned and boned chicken thighs	2	Tbsp. cold butter, cut up
1	Tbsp. Greek seasoning	1	Tbsp. red wine vinegar
2	Tbsp. olive oil	¼	tsp. salt
2	medium zucchini, chopped	¼	tsp. pepper
½	cup diced onion		

1. Prepare potatoes according to package directions. Keep warm.

2. Meanwhile, sprinkle chicken with Greek seasoning. Cook chicken in hot oil in large skillet over medium-high heat 7 to 8 minutes on each side or until done. Remove from skillet, and keep warm.

3. Reduce heat to medium. Add zucchini and onion to skillet, and sauté 2 to 3 minutes or until tender. Add tomatoes, and cook, stirring often, 7 to 10 minutes or until slightly thickened. Remove from heat, and stir in butter and next 3 ingredients.

4. Serve chicken over potatoes. Spoon sauce over chicken and potatoes. Serve immediately.

Note: We tested wtih Ore-Ida Steam n' Mash Cut Red Potatoes, Cavender's All Purpose Greek Seasoning, and Hunt's Fire Roasted Tomatoes Diced With Garlic.

sidekick: **BALSAMIC-GLAZED GREEN BEANS** Microwave 1 (12-oz.) package fresh green beans, trimmed, according to package directions. While beans cook, melt 1 Tbsp. butter in a large skillet over medium heat. Add 3 Tbsp. minced shallots and 2 garlic cloves, minced; cook, stirring constantly, 2 minutes. Stir in ¼ cup balsamic vinegar, ½ tsp. salt, and ¼ tsp. freshly ground pepper; cook 1 minute. Add beans, tossing to coat.

savvy secret
from Vanessa:

If you have little ones, chop the zucchini and onion in this dish into smaller pieces; they will never know it's there. Serving the chicken over mashed potatoes makes this one-dish recipe hearty and filling.

kid favorite

Chicken Cutlets with Pecan Sauce

MAKES 4 SERVINGS
HANDS-ON TIME: 23 MIN.   **TOTAL TIME: 23 MIN.**

½	cup pecan halves		3	Tbsp. olive oil
¼	cup butter, divided		½	cup chicken broth
4	chicken cutlets (about 1¼ lb.)		1	Tbsp. brown sugar
1	tsp. salt		2	Tbsp. cider vinegar
½	tsp. pepper		½	tsp. dried thyme
3	Tbsp. all-purpose flour		Garnish: fresh thyme	

1. Heat pecans and 2 Tbsp. butter in a large nonstick skillet over medium-low heat, stirring often, 2 to 3 minutes or until toasted and fragrant. Remove from skillet.

2. Sprinkle chicken with salt and pepper. Dredge in flour.

3. Cook chicken in hot oil in skillet over medium heat 3 to 4 minutes on each side or until golden brown and done. Transfer to a serving platter. Top with pecans.

4. Add chicken broth to skillet, and cook 2 minutes, stirring to loosen particles from bottom of skillet. Add brown sugar, vinegar, and dried thyme, and cook 3 to 4 minutes or until sugar is melted and sauce is slightly thickened. Whisk in remaining 2 Tbsp. butter. Serve sauce over chicken. Garnish, if desired.

sidekick: **GARLIC-PEPPER MIXED VEGETABLE**S Cook 1 (11-oz.) package frozen steam-in-bag mixed vegetables according to package directions. Toss with 1 tsp. freshly ground garlic-pepper seasoning.

table talk: Go out for dinner tonight—out of the kitchen, that is. And set up dinner on the coffee table or a picnic supper on the porch. See what new conversations might spark from changing the dinner location.

Grilled Chicken with Fresh Corn Cakes

MAKES 4 SERVINGS
HANDS-ON TIME: 15 MIN.   **TOTAL TIME: 56 MIN.**

3	lemons	1	Tbsp. olive oil
2	garlic cloves, pressed	1	(6-oz.) package buttermilk
⅓	cup olive oil		cornbread and muffin mix
1	tsp. Dijon mustard	¼	cup chopped fresh basil
¼	tsp. pepper	8	cooked thick hickory-
1½	tsp. salt, divided		smoked bacon slices,
3	skinned and boned chicken		crumbled
	breasts	2	cups loosely packed arugula
3	ears fresh corn, husks removed	½	cup chopped tomato

1. Preheat grill to 350° to 400° (medium-high) heat. Grate 1 Tbsp. zest from lemons. Cut in half; squeeze juice into a measuring cup to equal ¼ cup.

2. Whisk together lemon zest, lemon juice, garlic, next 3 ingredients, and 1 tsp. salt. Reserve ¼ cup lemon mixture. Pour remaining mixture in a large zip-top plastic freezer bag; add chicken. Seal and chill 15 minutes, turning once. Remove chicken from marinade, discarding marinade.

3. Brush corn with 1 Tbsp. olive oil; sprinkle with remaining ½ tsp. salt.

4. Grill chicken and corn at the same time, covered with grill lid, 20 minutes, turning chicken once and turning corn every 4 to 5 minutes. Remove chicken; cover. Hold each grilled cob upright on a cutting board, and carefully cut downward, cutting kernels from cob.

5. Stir together cornbread mix and ⅔ cup water until smooth. Stir in basil and 1 cup grilled corn kernels. Pour ¼ cup batter for each cake onto a hot, lightly greased griddle. Cook 3 to 4 minutes or until tops are covered with bubbles and edges look cooked; turn and cook other side.

6. Thinly slice chicken. To serve, place 2 corn cakes on each plate, top with chicken and bacon. Toss arugula with reserved lemon mixture. Place arugula on bacon; sprinkle with corn kernels and chopped tomato.

flavor profile: fresh corn

Always buy fresh ears of corn in their husks. The husk is essential because it helps retain the corn's natural moisture, making it taste fresher. Look for green husks that don't appear dry. Then pull back an edge of the husk to check that the kernels are plump, tight, and a vivid color; they should not appear dull, wrinkled, or dry.

Chicken with Couscous, Tomatoes, and Hummus

MAKES 4 SERVINGS
HANDS-ON TIME: 30 MIN.   TOTAL TIME: 30 MIN.

- 1 (10-oz.) package plain couscous
- 4 (4- to 6-oz.) skinned and boned chicken breasts
- 2 Tbsp. olive oil, divided
- 1¼ tsp. salt, divided
- ½ tsp. pepper, divided
- 6 plum tomatoes, seeded and diced
- 1 garlic clove, minced
- 3 Tbsp. chopped fresh basil
- 2 Tbsp. minced red onion
- 1 Tbsp. lemon juice
- 1 (7-oz.) container hummus
- 4 pita bread rounds, cut into quarters

1. Prepare couscous according to package directions.

2. Brush chicken with I Tbsp. oil; sprinkle with ¾ tsp. salt and ¼ tsp. pepper.

3. Cook chicken, covered, in a large grill pan or nonstick skillet over medium-high heat 8 to 10 minutes on each side or until done.

4. Meanwhile, combine tomatoes, next 4 ingredients, and remaining I Tbsp. oil, ½ tsp. salt, and ¼ tsp. pepper. Stir tomato mixture into prepared couscous.

5. Divide couscous mixture, hummus, and pita bread quarters among 4 serving plates; top each with I chicken breast.

time-saving tip:
Use kitchen scissors to quickly cut the pita bread into quarters.

healthy

Grilled Chicken Tacos

MAKES 4 TO 6 SERVINGS
HANDS-ON TIME: 20 MIN.   TOTAL TIME: 42 MIN.

3   Tbsp. olive oil
2   Tbsp. lime juice
4   tsp. Montreal chicken
      seasoning
1½   lb. chicken breast tenders
1   (8-oz.) container refrigerated
      fresh salsa
1   large mango, peeled and
      chopped

¼   cup chopped fresh cilantro
2   tsp. chipotle hot sauce
6   (6-inch) fajita-size flour
      tortillas, warmed
Toppings: crumbled queso fresco
      (fresh Mexican cheese),
      shredded romaine lettuce

1. Preheat grill to 300° to 350° (medium) heat. Combine first 3 ingredients in a zip-top plastic freezer bag; add chicken, turning to coat. Seal and chill 10 minutes, turning once.

2. Meanwhile, combine salsa and next 3 ingredients. Cover and chill until ready to serve.

3. Remove chicken from marinade, discarding marinade. Grill chicken, covered with grill lid, 6 minutes on each side or until done. Serve in flour tortillas with salsa mixture and desired toppings.

Note: We tested with McCormick Grill Mates Montreal Chicken Seasoning.

sidekick: **DRESSED-UP REFRIED BEANS** Preheat oven to 450°. Combine 2 (20.5-oz.) cans refried black beans, ½ (8-oz.) package whipped chive-flavored cream cheese, and ½ tsp. ground cumin in a 2-qt. baking dish. Top with 2 Tbsp. finely chopped red onion and 1 cup crumbled queso fresco (fresh Mexican cheese). Bake at 450° for 20 to 30 minutes or until cheese melts.

Lemon Chicken

MAKES 8 SERVINGS
HANDS-ON TIME: 30 MIN.   **TOTAL TIME: 30 MIN.**

4	skinned and boned chicken breasts (about 1½ lb.)
1	tsp. salt
½	tsp. pepper
⅓	cup all-purpose flour
4	Tbsp. butter, divided
2	Tbsp. olive oil
¼	cup chicken broth
¼	cup lemon juice
8	lemon slices
¼	cup chopped fresh flat-leaf parsley

Garnishes: lemon slices, sliced green onions

1. Cut each chicken breast in half lengthwise. Place chicken between 2 sheets of heavy-duty plastic wrap; flatten to ¼-inch thickness, using a rolling pin or flat side of a meat mallet. Sprinkle chicken with salt and pepper. Lightly dredge chicken in flour, shaking off excess.

2. Melt 1 Tbsp. butter with 1 Tbsp. olive oil in a large nonstick skillet over medium-high heat. Cook half of chicken in skillet 2 to 3 minutes on each side or until golden brown and done. Transfer chicken to a serving platter, and keep warm. Repeat procedure with 1 Tbsp. butter and remaining olive oil and chicken.

3. Add broth and lemon juice to skillet, and cook 1 to 2 minutes or until sauce is slightly thickened, stirring to loosen particles from bottom of skillet. Add 8 lemon slices. Remove skillet from heat; add parsley and remaining 2 Tbsp. butter, and stir until butter melts. Pour sauce over chicken. Serve immediately. Garnish, if desired.

sidekick: **OREGANO GREEN BEANS** Sauté 2 cups chopped onion in 2 Tbsp. olive oil in a Dutch oven over medium heat 8 minutes or until tender. Add 1 garlic clove, minced; cook, stirring often, 4 minutes or until garlic is tender and golden brown. Add 1 lb. fresh green beans, trimmed; 1 (14½-oz.) can diced tomatoes, drained; ½ cup vegetable or chicken broth; 1 Tbsp. chopped fresh oregano; 1 Tbsp. chopped fresh parsley; ¾ tsp. salt; and ½ tsp. pepper. Bring to a boil; reduce heat to low, cover, and simmer 10 minutes or until beans are tender. Stir in 1 Tbsp. fresh lemon juice. Transfer to a serving dish; sprinkle with ½ cup crumbled feta.

Chicken-and-Spinach Enchiladas

MAKES 6 SERVINGS
HANDS-ON TIME: 15 MIN.   TOTAL TIME: 50 MIN.

- 1 (10-oz.) package frozen chopped spinach, thawed
- 1 (16-oz.) jar medium chunky salsa, divided
- 2 (10-oz.) cans mild red enchilada sauce
- 1 (8-oz.) package cream cheese*
- 2½ cups shredded or chopped deli-roasted chicken
- 10 (8-inch) soft taco-size flour tortillas
- 1 (8-oz.) package shredded Mexican four-cheese blend
- Toppings: shredded lettuce, chopped fresh cilantro, chopped red onion, halved grape tomatoes

time-saving tip: Make a few pans of enchiladas, and keep them in the freezer for busy days. Line each dish with heavy-duty aluminum foil. Cover and freeze finished casserole 2 to 3 hours. Lift the frozen casserole from the dish and freeze in a zip-top plastic freezer bag. Store up to 3 months.

1. Preheat oven to 350°. Lightly grease a 13- x 9-inch baking dish. Drain spinach well, pressing between paper towels.

2. Stir together ¼ cup salsa and enchilada sauce.

3. Microwave cream cheese in a medium-size microwave-safe bowl at HIGH 1 minute or until very soft. Add spinach, chicken, and remaining salsa; stir until blended.

4. Spoon a heaping ⅓ cupful chicken mixture down center of each tortilla. Roll up tortillas, and place, seam sides down, in prepared baking dish. Pour enchilada sauce mixture over top of rolled tortillas; sprinkle with shredded cheese.

5. Bake at 350° for 30 minutes or until bubbly. Let stand 5 minutes. Serve with desired toppings.

*⅓-less-fat cream cheese may be substituted.

Note: We tested with Tostitos All-Natural Chunky Salsa and Old El Paso Mild Red Enchilada Sauce.

sidekick: **CILANTRO RICE** Heat 2 (10-oz.) packages frozen brown rice according to package directions. Transfer rice to a medium bowl, and stir in ⅔ cup bottled taco sauce and ½ cup chopped fresh cilantro.

healthy

Mediterranean Chicken Salad

MAKES 6 SERVINGS
HANDS-ON TIME: 15 MIN.   TOTAL TIME: 35 MIN.

2 cups boiling water	½ cup bottled Caesar dressing
1 cup uncooked bulgur wheat	¼ cup finely chopped red
1½ tsp. salt, divided	onion
3 cups chopped cooked	1 (4-oz.) package crumbled
chicken	feta
1 cup grape tomatoes, halved	1 medium cucumber, peeled
2 garlic cloves, pressed	and chopped
¾ cup chopped fresh	
parsley	

1. Combine boiling water, bulgur wheat, and 1 tsp. salt. Cover and let stand 20 minutes or until tender. Drain and rinse with cold water.

2. Combine bulgur wheat mixture, chicken, next 7 ingredients, and remaining ½ tsp. salt.

Mediterranean Chicken Salad with Rice: Omit boiling water. Reduce salt to ½ tsp. Substitute 1 (6-oz.) package long-grain and wild rice mix for bulgur wheat. Prepare rice according to package directions. Proceed with recipe as directed in Step 2.

time-saving tip: The fastest way to chop parsley is to place a bunch of parsley into a small bowl. Cut the parsley with a pair of kitchen shears until the parsley is completely chopped.

for company
Baked Chicken Risotto

MAKES 4 SERVINGS
HANDS-ON TIME: 20 MIN.   TOTAL TIME: 1 HR.

3   Tbsp. butter
1   cup minced sweet onion
2   garlic cloves, pressed
1   cup Arborio rice (short-grain)
¼   cup dry white wine
4   cups chicken broth
1   (14-oz.) can quartered
    artichoke hearts, drained

3   cups chopped cooked
    chicken
2   medium zucchini, coarsely
    chopped (about 2 cups)
½   tsp. freshly ground pepper
½   cup grated Parmesan cheese
¼   cup chopped fresh parsley
1   tsp. lemon zest

1. Preheat oven to 425°. Melt butter in a Dutch oven over medium-high heat; add onion and garlic, and sauté 5 minutes. Add rice, and cook, stirring often, 2 minutes or until golden brown. Add wine, and cook 2 to 3 minutes or until wine is absorbed. Add chicken broth. Bring to a boil, cover, and transfer to oven. Bake 20 minutes.

2. Remove rice from oven, and stir in artichokes and next 3 ingredients. Cover and bake 10 minutes. Remove from oven, and let stand 5 minutes. Stir in cheese and remaining ingredients. Serve immediately.

sidekick: **SAUTÉED GREEN BEANS WITH BACON** Cook 3 slices of bacon, cut into 1-inch pieces, and ⅓ cup chopped onion in a large skillet over medium heat, stirring often, 6 minutes or until browned. Transfer to a plate, reserving drippings in skillet. Cook 1 (16-oz.) package frozen whole or cut green beans in hot drippings, stirring often, 8 minutes or to desired degree of tenderness. Toss in onions and bacon.

savvy secret
from Vanessa:

Choose lemons that are fragrant, bright, and colorful. Avoid those with bruises and brown spots. When zesting a lemon, be sure not to grate the pith (the white portion) because of its bitter taste.

healthy

Quick Turkey Chili

MAKES 6 TO 8 SERVINGS
HANDS-ON TIME: 30 MIN.   TOTAL TIME: 1 HR., 5 MIN.

1	medium onion, chopped	1	(16-oz.) can red kidney beans,
1	Tbsp. vegetable oil		drained and rinsed
2	garlic cloves, chopped	1	cup chicken broth
1	lb. ground turkey	1	cup beer*
2	Tbsp. chili powder	1	tsp. salt
2	tsp. ground cumin	½	tsp. pepper
3	Tbsp. tomato paste	¼	cup chopped fresh cilantro
1	(28-oz.) can diced tomatoes		

1. Sauté chopped onion in hot oil in a large Dutch oven over medium-high heat 5 minutes or until tender; add garlic, and sauté 1 minute.

2. Add turkey, chili powder, and cumin, and cook, stirring often, 8 minutes or until meat crumbles and is no longer pink. Stir in tomato paste, and cook 2 minutes. Add tomatoes and next 5 ingredients. Bring mixture to a boil; cover, reduce heat to low, and simmer, stirring occasionally, 30 minutes. Stir in cilantro.

* Chicken broth may be substituted.

sidekick: **GRILLED THREE-CHEESE SANDWICHES** Stir together ¼ cup softened butter and 1 Tbsp. grated Parmesan cheese in a small bowl. Spread 1½ tsp. butter mixture on 1 side of 8 Italian bread slices. Place 4 bread slices, buttered sides down, on wax paper. Top each bread slice with 1 (¾-oz.) provolone cheese slice and 1 (¾-oz.) mozzarella cheese slice; top with remaining bread slices, buttered sides up. Cook sandwiches, in batches, on a hot griddle or in a nonstick skillet over medium heat, gently pressing with a spatula, 4 minutes on each side or until golden brown and cheese is melted. Slice sandwiches in half diagonally.

don't drive through, drive home

These quick-to-make favorites taste so much better than fast food

Tuscan Pasta with Tomato-Basil Cream

MAKES 4 TO 6 SERVINGS
HANDS-ON TIME: 15 MIN.   TOTAL TIME: 15 MIN.

1 (20-oz.) package refrigerated four-cheese ravioli*	2 medium-size fresh tomatoes, chopped**
1 (16-oz.) jar sun-dried tomato Alfredo sauce	½ cup chopped fresh basil
2 Tbsp. white wine	⅓ cup freshly grated Parmesan cheese

1. Prepare pasta according to package directions. Keep warm.

2. Meanwhile, pour Alfredo sauce into a medium saucepan. Pour wine into sauce jar; cover tightly, and shake well. Stir wine mixture into saucepan. Stir in chopped tomatoes and chopped basil, and cook over medium-low heat 5 minutes or until thoroughly heated. Toss cream sauce with pasta, and top with ⅓ cup grated Parmesan cheese.

* 1 (20-oz.) package three-cheese tortellini may be substituted.

** 1 (14.5-oz.) can petite diced tomatoes, well drained, may be substituted.

Note: We tested with Buitoni Four Cheese Ravioli and Classico Sun-dried Tomato Alfredo Pasta Sauce.

sidekick: **SAUTÉED ZUCCHINI SPEARS** Cut 3 medium zucchini in half lengthwise; cut each half crosswise into 2 pieces. Cut each piece into 3 spears. Heat 1½ tsp. olive oil in a large nonstick skillet over medium-high heat; add zucchini and ½ cup coarsely chopped onion. Sauté 5 to 6 minutes or until vegetables are lightly browned. Sprinkle with salt and pepper to taste; toss well.

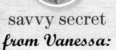

savvy secret
from Vanessa:

When storing a bunch of fresh herbs, wrap the stems in a damp paper towel, and place them in a zip-top freezer bag in the refrigerator. Wash herbs just before using; pat them dry with a paper towel.

healthy

Wild Mushroom Agnolotti with Wilted Greens

MAKES 4 SERVINGS
HANDS-ON TIME: 25 MIN.   TOTAL TIME: 25 MIN.

1	(9-oz.) package refrigerated wild mushroom agnolotti
4	bacon slices, chopped
1	small onion, chopped
1	garlic clove, minced
¼	cup dry white wine
1	to 2 Tbsp. balsamic vinegar
½	cup chicken broth
½	cup frozen peas
2	plum tomatoes, chopped
½	(5.5-oz.) package spring greens and baby spinach mix
½	cup freshly grated Parmesan cheese

1. Prepare pasta according to package directions. Keep warm.

2. Meanwhile, cook bacon in a large skillet over medium-high heat 6 to 8 minutes or until crisp; remove bacon, and drain on paper towels, reserving 2 Tbsp. drippings in skillet. Sauté onion in hot drippings 3 minutes or until tender. Stir in garlic, and sauté 1 minute. Stir in wine and vinegar, and cook 2 minutes, stirring to loosen particles from bottom of skillet.

3. Stir in chicken broth, next 2 ingredients, and agnolotti, and cook 2 to 3 minutes or until thoroughly heated. Serve over salad greens, and sprinkle with bacon and Parmesan cheese.

Note: Agnolotti look like ravioli. We tested with Buitoni Wild Mushroom Agnolotti and Fresh Express 50/50 Mix.

sidekick: **BRUSSELS SPROUTS WITH BACON DRESSING** Cook 4 bacon slices in a Dutch oven over medium heat 10 minutes or until crisp. Remove bacon, and drain on paper towels, reserving drippings in Dutch oven. Crumble bacon. Add 1 (14-oz.) can chicken broth, 1 Tbsp. brown sugar, and 1 tsp. salt to drippings; bring to a boil. Stir in 1½ lb. Brussels sprouts. Cover and cook 6 to 8 minutes or until tender. Transfer Brussels sprouts to a serving bowl using a slotted spoon, and sprinkle with bacon. Serve immediately.

table talk: A quick and easy pasta dish makes a great book club night supper. Select a book that everyone will enjoy. Then pick a night to discuss it over dinner. Grab some bakery brownies to continue the conversation over dessert, hot chocolate, and coffee.

Black Bean Chili

MAKES 8 SERVINGS
HANDS-ON TIME: 10 MIN.   TOTAL TIME: 25 MIN.

3	(15-oz.) cans black beans	½	tsp. pepper
1	large sweet onion, chopped	¼	tsp. salt
1	(12-oz.) package meatless burger crumbles	1	(14-oz.) can low-sodium fat-free chicken broth
2	Tbsp. vegetable oil	2	(14.5-oz.) cans petite diced tomatoes with jalapeños
4	tsp. chili powder		Garnish: sliced jalapeño peppers
1	tsp. ground cumin		

1. Drain and rinse 2 cans black beans. (Do not drain third can.)

2. Sauté chopped onion and burger crumbles in hot oil in a large Dutch oven over medium heat 6 minutes. Stir in chili powder and next 3 ingredients; sauté 1 minute. Stir in chicken broth, diced tomatoes, and drained and undrained beans. Bring to a boil over medium-high heat; cover, reduce heat to low, and simmer 10 minutes. Garnish, if desired.

Note: We tested with Boca Meatless Ground Crumbles for meatless burger crumbles. For additional flavorful toppings, try sour cream, shredded Cheddar cheese, lime wedges, chopped fresh cilantro, chopped tomatoes, and corn chips.

Meaty Black Bean Chili: Substitute 1 lb. ground round for meatless burger crumbles, sautéing ground round with onion 10 minutes or until meat is no longer pink. Omit vegetable oil. Proceed as directed.

sidekick: **GRILLED PIMIENTO CHEESE** Spread deli pimiento cheese on 1 side of a white bread slice; top with another bread slice. Lightly spread both sides of sandwich with mayonnaise. Repeat with remaining pimiento cheese for desired number of sandwiches. Cook, in batches, on a hot griddle or large nonstick skillet over medium heat 4 to 5 minutes on each side or until golden brown and cheese melts.

Fettuccine with Green Peas and Fresh Mint

MAKES 3 TO 4 SERVINGS
HANDS-ON TIME: 15 MIN.   **TOTAL TIME: 30 MIN.**

1	(9-oz.) package refrigerated fettuccine	2	garlic cloves, minced
1	Tbsp. butter	1	tsp. lemon zest
¾	cup frozen baby sweet peas	¼	tsp. salt
⅔	cup half-and-half	¼	tsp. pepper
½	cup ricotta cheese		Garnish: fresh shaved Parmesan cheese, fresh mint sprig
¼	cup chopped fresh mint		
¼	cup freshly grated Parmesan cheese		

1. Prepare pasta according to package directions. Keep warm.

2. Melt butter in a large skillet over medium heat. Add peas and next 8 ingredients. Reduce heat to low, and cook, stirring constantly, 5 minutes or until cheese is melted. Stir in pasta, and serve immediately. Garnish, if desired.

flavor profile: mint

This versatile herb can be used in both sweet and savory dishes. It comes in many varieties, but spearmint is the preferred choice for cooking. Its gray-green leaves are fuzzy, making them very different from the darker stemmed, rounded leaves of peppermint.

sidekick: **BALSAMIC-GLAZED BROCCOLI** Cook 1 (12-oz.) package fresh broccoli florets according to package directions; keep warm. Combine 1 Tbsp. butter, 1 tsp. lemon zest, 1 tsp. fresh lemon juice, 1 tsp. balsamic vinegar, and ¼ tsp. salt in a small microwave-safe bowl. Microwave at HIGH 30 seconds or until butter melts. Pour butter mixture over broccoli; toss gently to coat.

for company

Steak Salad with Roasted Sweet Potato Fries

MAKES 8 SERVINGS
HANDS-ON TIME: 30 MIN.   **TOTAL TIME: 30 MIN.**

½	lb. fresh green beans	2	rib-eye steaks (about 1¼ lb.)
1	(20-oz.) package frozen sweet potato fries	2	garlic cloves, pressed
1	medium-size sweet onion, cut into wedges	1	large head romaine lettuce, torn
	Vegetable cooking spray	4	plum tomatoes, chopped
2	Tbsp. olive oil, divided	½	cup smoked almonds, coarsely chopped
1½	tsp. salt, divided	½	cup bottled peppercorn Ranch dressing
¾	tsp. pepper, divided		

1. Preheat oven to 475°. Cook beans in boiling salted water to cover 5 minutes or until crisp-tender; drain. Plunge into ice water to stop the cooking process; drain.

2. Place sweet potatoes and onion in a large aluminum foil-lined jelly-roll pan coated with cooking spray. Drizzle potato mixture with 1 Tbsp. oil, and sprinkle with ½ tsp. salt and ¼ tsp. pepper. Toss to coat.

3. Bake at 475° for 25 to 30 minutes or until potatoes and onion are tender and golden, stirring occasionally.

4. Meanwhile, rub steaks with garlic and remaining 1 Tbsp. oil, 1 tsp. salt, and ½ tsp. pepper.

5. Heat a grill pan over medium-high heat; cook steaks in pan 4 to 5 minutes on each side or to desired degree of doneness. Let stand 10 minutes.

6. Toss together lettuce, tomatoes, almonds, and green beans. Thinly slice steak, and place on salad. Drizzle with salad dressing. Serve with potato mixture.

time-saving tip:
Substitute 1 (16-oz.) package of shredded romaine lettuce for the head of romaine lettuce.

Ginger Flank Steak with Edamame Rice

MAKES 4 SERVINGS
HANDS-ON TIME: 30 MIN.   TOTAL TIME: 30 MIN.

1 Tbsp. grated fresh ginger	½ tsp. pepper
1 Tbsp. olive oil	½ lime
6 Tbsp. chopped fresh cilantro, divided	2 (8.5-oz.) pouches ready-to-serve basmati rice
1 (1-lb.) flank steak	2 cups fully cooked shelled frozen edamame, thawed
1 tsp. salt	

1. Preheat grill to 400° to 450° (high) heat. Stir together ginger, oil, and 2 Tbsp. cilantro in a small bowl. Rub cilantro mixture on steak. Sprinkle with salt and pepper.

2. Grill steak, covered with grill lid, 6 to 7 minutes on each side or to desired degree of doneness. Remove from grill; squeeze juice from lime over steak. Cover loosely with foil, and let stand 10 minutes.

3. Meanwhile, prepare rice according to package directions, and stir in edamame and remaining 4 Tbsp. cilantro. Cut steak across the grain into thin slices; serve over rice.

flavor profile: edamame

These fresh soybeans have a buttery, nutty flavor and wonderfully crisp texture. They also make a fun—and addictive—snack food. You simply use your teeth to squeeze the beans out of the salted pods, which are picked while young and look like large, fuzzy sugar snap peas. The beans themselves are similar in color to fresh fava or lima beans. The beans—which are sold frozen as well as fully cooked and ready to eat—are available at most grocery stores.

healthy

Cilantro Flank Steak

MAKES 6 SERVINGS
HANDS-ON TIME: 24 MIN. **TOTAL TIME: 24 MIN.**

1½	lb. flank steak	2	Tbsp. fresh lime juice
5	Tbsp. olive oil, divided	2	garlic cloves, minced
1½	tsp. Montreal steak seasoning	½	tsp. salt
1½	cups firmly packed fresh cilantro leaves		

1. Brush steak with 1 Tbsp. oil; sprinkle with seasoning.

2. Heat a cast-iron grill pan over medium-high heat; cook steak in pan 7 to 9 minutes on each side or to desired degree of doneness.

3. Process cilantro, next 3 ingredients, and remaining 4 Tbsp. oil in a food processor until smooth. Cut steak diagonally across the grain into thin slices. Serve sauce with steak.

sidekick: **GARLIC RICE WITH CILANTRO AND CORN** Prepare 2 (8.5-oz.) packages ready-to-serve roasted garlic whole grain rice according to package directions. Stir in 1 (8-oz.) can sweet whole kernel corn, drained, and ¼ cup chopped fresh cilantro.

savvy secret
from Vanessa:

A grill pan is great alternative to grilling all kinds of meats. The key is not to turn the heat too high or you will burn your food.

kid favorite

Lamb Burgers

MAKES 6 SERVINGS
HANDS-ON TIME: 30 MIN.   **TOTAL TIME: 30 MIN.**

1 cup fat-free Greek yogurt	¼ cup finely chopped fresh mint
½ cup peeled, grated cucumber	
1 tsp. finely chopped fresh mint	1 Tbsp. finely chopped fresh oregano
3 garlic cloves, pressed and divided	1 Tbsp. whole grain mustard
1¾ tsp. salt, divided	6 hamburger buns
2 lb. ground lamb	Toppings: Bibb lettuce, sliced tomatoes, sliced red onion, dill pickle chips
¼ cup minced red onion	

1. Preheat grill to 350° to 400° (medium-high) heat. Stir together first 3 ingredients, 1 pressed garlic clove, and ½ tsp. salt. Cover and chill until ready to serve.

2. Gently combine lamb, next 4 ingredients, and remaining 2 pressed garlic cloves and 1¼ tsp. salt. Shape mixture into 6 (4-inch) patties.

3. Grill patties, covered with grill lid, 5 to 6 minutes on each side or to desired degree of doneness. Serve burgers on buns with yogurt sauce and desired toppings

sidekick: Serve this with deli tabbouleh salad.

table talk: Make burger night family game night. Pull out your favorite games, whether they be Pictionary, Scrabble, Monopoly, or simply a deck of cards. In the spring, you can even turn game night into a picnic and play an outdoor game such as tag, kickball, or basketball.

Pork Tenderloin Tacos with Radish-Avocado Salsa

MAKES 4 SERVINGS
HANDS-ON TIME: 25 MIN.   TOTAL TIME: 25 MIN.

SALSA

1	(6-oz.) package radishes
½	small red onion, diced
1	avocado, diced
1	jalapeño pepper, seeded and minced
¼	cup chopped fresh cilantro
2	Tbsp. lime juice
¼	tsp. salt

TACOS

2	Tbsp. brown sugar
3	Tbsp. olive oil
2	tsp. salt
1	tsp. ground cumin
½	tsp. ground red pepper
1	lb. pork tenderloin, cut into 1-inch cubes
8	(6-inch) fajita-size corn or flour tortillas, warmed

Garnish: lime quarters

1. Prepare Salsa: Process radishes in a food processor until finely chopped. Stir together radishes, onion, and next 5 ingredients; cover and chill salsa until ready to serve.

2. Prepare Tacos: Stir together brown sugar and next 4 ingredients. Toss pork with brown sugar mixture. Heat grill pan over medium-high heat; cook pork, in 2 batches, 2½ minutes on each side or until done. Serve pork in warm tortillas with salsa. Garnish, if desired.

time-saving tip:
To easily remove the pit from avocados, use a 6- to 8-inch chef's knife. Insert it into the top where the stem was (it will be a darker area), and gently press down until you reach the pit. Scoop the pit out gently with a spoon.

Grilled Basil-and-Garlic Pork Chops

MAKES 6 SERVINGS
HANDS-ON TIME: 15 MIN.   TOTAL TIME: 15 MIN.

1	tsp. salt	½	tsp. garlic powder
1	tsp. pepper	6	(6- to 8-oz.) bone-in pork
1	tsp. dried basil		loin chops

1. Preheat grill to 350° to 400° (medium-high) heat. Combine first 4 ingredients; sprinkle over pork chops.

2. Grill pork, covered with grill lid, 5 to 7 minutes on each side or until done.

sidekick: **BASMATI RICE AND PEAS** Bring 2 cups chicken broth, 1 Tbsp. butter, and ½ tsp. salt to a boil over medium-high heat in a large saucepan. Stir in 1 cup basmati rice; cover, reduce heat to low, and simmer 20 minutes or until broth is absorbed and rice is tender. Remove from heat, and stir in 1 (15½-oz.) can black-eyed peas, drained and rinsed, and 1½ tsp. lemon zest, using a fork. Cover and let stand 5 minutes. Sprinkle with 2 green onions, thinly sliced.

flavor profile: basmati rice

Sometimes called "popcorn rice," this long-grain variety is highly regarded for its fragrance, taste, and slender shape. True basmati is grown in India and Pakistan, although many hybrids are grown elsewhere, including the United States.

savvy secret
from Vanessa:

Today's pork is pretty lean so we recommend heartier chops that are at least ½ to 1 inch thick. This will give you a moister pork chop. This dish is easy enough for a weeknight supper, but elegant enough for company.

Okra-and-Corn Maque Choux

MAKES 8 SERVINGS
HANDS-ON TIME: 28 MIN.   TOTAL TIME: 28 MIN.

¼ lb. spicy smoked sausage, diced	3 cups fresh corn kernels
½ cup chopped sweet onion	1 cup sliced fresh okra
½ cup chopped green bell pepper	1 cup peeled, seeded, and diced tomato (½ lb.)
2 garlic cloves, minced	Salt and freshly ground pepper to taste

1. Sauté sausage in a large skillet over medium-high heat 3 minutes or until browned. Add onion, bell pepper, and garlic, and sauté 5 minutes or until tender. Add corn, okra, and tomato; cook, stirring often, 10 minutes. Season with salt and pepper to taste.

Note: We tested with Conecuh Original Spicy and Hot Smoked Sausage.

sidekick: **CORNBREAD MUFFINS** Preheat oven to 450°. Stir together 2 cups self-rising white cornmeal mix and ½ cup sugar in a large bowl; make a well in center of mixture. Whisk together 5 large eggs, 1 (16-oz.) container sour cream, and ½ cup butter; add to cornmeal, stirring just until dry ingredients are moistened. Spoon batter into 2 lightly greased 12-cup muffin pans, filling three-fourths full. Bake at 450° for 15 to 17 minutes or until tops are golden brown. Cool in pan on a wire rack 5 minutes.

savvy secret
from Vanessa:

Seeding tomatoes gets rid of excess liquid and the bitter seeds that can sometimes alter a dish's flavor. To seed, cut the tomato in half horizontally. Using a spoon, scoop the seeds and pulp away from the flesh, and discard.

Ham Steak with Orange Glaze

MAKES 6 SERVINGS
HANDS-ON TIME: 10 MIN.   TOTAL TIME: 20 MIN.

1 (2½-lb.) package fully cooked, bone-in (½-inch-thick) center-cut ham steak	¼ cup golden raisins
1 cup orange juice	1 Tbsp. Dijon mustard
1 (8-oz.) can pineapple tidbits in juice	1 tsp. cornstarch
	1 Tbsp. cold water

1. Rinse ham, and pat dry.

2. Cook ham in a lightly greased skillet over medium-high heat 3 to 4 minutes on each side or until thoroughly heated. Remove ham, reserving drippings in skillet.

3. Stir in orange juice, and cook 2 minutes, stirring to loosen browned particles from bottom of skillet. Stir in pineapple and next 2 ingredients. Stir together cornstarch and 1 Tbsp. cold water; add to orange juice mixture. Bring to a boil; cook, stirring constantly, 1 minute. Serve sauce with ham.

sidekick: **ROASTED VEGETABLES** Preheat oven to 450°. Peel 3 medium-size sweet potatoes (about 1½ lb.), and cut into ½-inch cubes. Cut 1 yellow bell pepper into 1-inch pieces. Combine sweet potatoes; bell pepper; 1 medium-size onion, coarsely chopped; 2 Tbsp. olive oil; 1 tsp. salt; 1 tsp. ground cinnamon; and ¼ tsp. pepper in a large zip-top plastic freezer bag; seal bag, and turn until vegetables are coated. Remove vegetable mixture from bag, and place in a single layer in a lightly greased 15- x 10-inch jelly-roll pan. Bake for 30 to 35 minutes or until sweet potatoes are tender.

Apple-Chicken Sausage with Apricot-Pepper Relish

MAKES 6 SERVINGS
HANDS-ON TIME: 18 MIN.   TOTAL TIME: 22 MIN.

½ cup chicken broth

¼ cup apricot preserves

1 Tbsp. apple cider vinegar

2 (12-oz.) packages smoked chicken-and-apple sausage links, cut in half lengthwise

1 Tbsp. olive oil

2 large red bell peppers, cut into thin strips

1 medium onion, thinly sliced

savvy secret
from Vanessa:

1. Whisk together chicken broth, preserves, and cider vinegar.

2. Cook sausage, in batches, in hot oil in a nonstick skillet over medium-high heat 3 to 5 minutes or until browned. Add peppers and onion; sauté 2 minutes. Add broth mixture, and reduce heat to medium; cover and cook 4 minutes. Serve with a slotted spoon.

sidekick: **CREAMY GRITS** Bring 2 (14-oz.) cans chicken broth and 2 cups milk to a boil in a saucepan over medium-high heat; reduce heat to low, and whisk in 1 cup uncooked regular grits. Cook, whisking occasionally, 15 to 20 minutes or until thickened and creamy.

If you plan to use the bell peppers within a day or two, keep them at room temperature for better flavor. You can also store them in a plastic bag in the refrigerator for up to one week. Be sure to wash and cut the peppers just before using them.

healthy
Tomato-Chicken Salad

MAKES 4 TO 6 SERVINGS
HANDS-ON TIME: 20 MIN.   **TOTAL TIME: 30 MIN.**

1	lemon	¼	cup sliced green onion
2	lb. assorted tomatoes, halved or chopped	¼	cup loosely packed fresh basil leaves
3	cups chopped cooked chicken	2	Tbsp. olive oil
1	large English cucumber, sliced	1	tsp. salt
½	cup chopped fresh flat-leaf parsley	½	tsp. freshly ground pepper
		½	cup crumbled feta cheese

1. Grate zest from lemon to equal 2 tsp.; squeeze juice from lemon to equal 2 Tbsp. Combine lemon zest, juice, tomatoes, and next 8 ingredients in a large bowl. Let stand 10 minutes. Toss with crumbled feta just before serving.

sidekick: **GRILLED BRUSCHETTA** Preheat grill to 400° to 450° (high) heat. Rub 6 (1-inch-thick) ciabatta or French bread baguette slices with a garlic clove; brush with extra virgin olive oil. Grill bread 1 to 2 minutes on each side or until toasted.

savvy secret
from Vanessa:

To get the most juice out of a fresh lemon, bring it to room temperature, and then use the palm of your hand to roll it on a countertop for a few times, applying a bit of pressure.
Cut the fruit in half, and then squeeze. Or, for easier work, use a handheld press to release the most juice while safely trapping the seeds. Place the lemon half, cut side down, in the press, and lower the handle.

healthy

Spring Chicken Cobb Salad

MAKES 4 SERVINGS   HANDS-ON TIME: 23 MIN.
TOTAL TIME: 28 MIN., INCLUDING VINAIGRETTE

1	large sweet onion	1	cup drained and chopped
2	tsp. olive oil		jarred roasted red-bell
¼	tsp. salt		peppers
¼	tsp. pepper	4	fully cooked bacon slices,
1	(5-oz.) package arugula		chopped
2	cups chopped or shredded	4	oz. crumbled goat cheese
	roasted chicken		Yogurt-Basil Vinaigrette
2	avocados, sliced		

1. Cut onion into ¼-inch wedges. Brush with olive oil, and sprinkle with salt and pepper. Heat a grill pan over medium-high heat; cook onion slices 4 to 5 minutes on each side or until lightly charred and tender.

2. Arrange arugula on a serving platter; top with onions, chicken, and next 4 ingredients. Serve with Yogurt-Basil Vinaigrette.

Salmon Cobb Salad: Omit chicken. Season 4 (4-oz.) salmon fillets with ¾ tsp. salt and ¼ tsp. pepper. Cook salmon, covered, in 1 Tbsp. hot olive oil in a large skillet over medium heat 8 to 10 minutes on each side or until done. Proceed with recipe as directed.

yogurt-basil vinaigrette

MAKES 1 CUP
HANDS-ON TIME: 5 MIN.   TOTAL TIME: 5 MIN.

½	cup plain fat-free yogurt	1	Tbsp. honey
¼	cup olive oil	½	tsp. salt
2	Tbsp. chopped fresh basil	⅛	tsp. pepper
2	Tbsp. red wine vinegar		

1. Whisk together all ingredients. Serve immediately, or cover and chill up to 8 hours. If chilled, let stand at room temperature 30 minutes before serving.

kid favorite

Chicken-Fried Chicken

MAKES 6 SERVINGS
HANDS-ON TIME: 30 MIN.   **TOTAL TIME: 30 MIN.**

6 (6-oz.) skinned and boned chicken breasts, cubed	2 large eggs, lightly beaten
1¾ tsp. salt	¼ cup milk
½ tsp. pepper	1 cup all-purpose flour
	Vegetable oil

1. Sprinkle chicken with salt and pepper. Combine eggs and milk in a shallow dish.

2. Dip chicken in egg mixture; dredge in flour, shaking off excess.

3. Pour oil to a depth of 1½ inches into a Dutch oven or large deep skillet; heat over medium heat. Fry chicken, in batches, 4 to 5 minutes on each side or until done. Place chicken on a wire rack in a jelly-roll pan, and keep warm in a 225° oven.

sidekick: **GARLIC MASHED POTATOES** Microwave 1 (24-oz.) package frozen steam-and-mash potatoes according to package directions. Transfer cooked potatoes to a large bowl, and stir in ⅓ cup buttermilk; 2 garlic cloves, finely chopped; ½ tsp. salt; ½ tsp. pepper; and 2 Tbsp. butter. Mash to desired consistency.

time-saving tip: Ask your butcher to cube chicken breasts.

time-saving tip: Use kitchen shears to quickly cut the Canadian bacon into thin strips.

kid favorite

Easy Skillet Cordon Bleu

MAKES 4 TO 6 SERVINGS
HANDS ON TIME: 10 MIN.   TOTAL TIME: 20 MIN.

½ cup Italian-seasoned breadcrumbs	1 Tbsp. olive oil
1 tsp. pepper	8 Canadian bacon slices, cut into thin strips
½ tsp. salt	4 (¾- or 1-oz.) Swiss cheese slices, halved
8 chicken tenders (about 1 lb.)	
1 Tbsp. butter	

1. Preheat broiler with oven rack 5½ inches from heat. Combine breadcrumbs and next 2 ingredients in a large zip-top plastic freezer bag. Add chicken to freezer bag. Seal bag, and shake to coat.

2. Melt butter with oil in an ovenproof skillet over medium heat. Cook chicken 3½ to 4 minutes on each side or until done. Arrange Canadian bacon strips over chicken in skillet, and top each with 1 cheese slice half. Broil 2 minutes or until cheese is melted.

sidekick: **ROASTED BROCCOLI** Preheat oven to 475°. Cut 1¼ lb. broccoli into 3-inch-long spears; cut thick stems in half lengthwise. Place in a single layer on a well-greased jelly-roll pan. Combine 1 Tbsp. olive oil and 1 garlic clove, pressed; drizzle broccoli with oil mixture, and toss well. Sprinkle with salt and pepper to taste. Bake for 14 minutes. Meanwhile, cook 3 Tbsp. sliced almonds in a small skillet over medium heat, stirring constantly, 2 minutes or until toasted. Sprinkle almonds over broccoli.

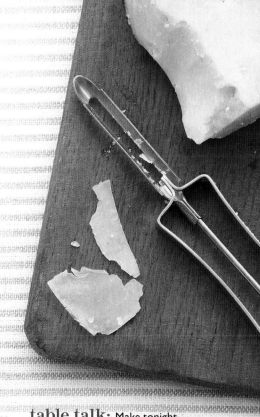

healthy

Balsamic-Garlic Chicken Breasts

MAKES 4 SERVINGS
HANDS-ON TIME: 22 MIN.   **TOTAL TIME: 22 MIN.**

4	(6-oz.) skinned and boned chicken breasts	½	cup chicken broth
		¼	cup balsamic vinegar
I	tsp. salt	I	Tbsp. fresh lemon juice
I	tsp. pepper	3	garlic cloves, chopped
2	Tbsp. butter	1½	tsp. honey
I	Tbsp. vegetable oil		Garnish: Parmesan curls

1. Sprinkle chicken breasts with salt and pepper.

2. Melt butter with oil in a large skillet over medium-high heat; add chicken, and cook 6 to 7 minutes on each side or until done. Remove chicken, and keep warm.

3. Add chicken broth and next 4 ingredients to skillet, and cook 5 minutes or until slightly thickened, stirring to loosen browned particles from bottom of skillet. Serve chicken with sauce.

sidekick: **PESTO-PARMESAN ORZO** Cook I cup orzo pasta according to package directions. Stir in ¼ cup refrigerated pesto. Sprinkle with freshly grated Parmesan cheese, if desired.

table talk: Make tonight wish night. Go around the table, and ask each person, "If you had one wish, what would it be and why?" Or make a game of it and have everyone write down his or her wishes and put them in a hat. Pass the hat around the table and let each person draw a wish out of the hat and read it aloud. Let folks at the table guess who put in that wish.

Turkey Piccata

MAKES 4 SERVINGS
HANDS-ON TIME: 30 MIN.   **TOTAL TIME: 30 MIN.**

1	lb. turkey cutlets*	2	Tbsp. olive oil
½	cup all-purpose flour	½	cup dry white wine
1	tsp. salt	⅓	cup fresh lemon juice
1	tsp. ground white pepper	1	Tbsp. drained capers
3	Tbsp. butter, divided	6	lemon slices, halved

1. Place turkey between 2 sheets of heavy-duty plastic wrap, and flatten to ¼-inch thickness, using a rolling pin or the flat side of a meat mallet.

2. Combine flour and next 2 ingredients in a shallow dish. Dredge cutlets in flour mixture.

3. Melt 1 Tbsp. butter with 1 Tbsp. olive oil in a large nonstick skillet over medium-high heat. Add half of turkey, and cook 2 to 3 minutes on each side or until golden brown. Remove from skillet, and place on a wire rack in a jelly-roll pan in a 200° oven to keep warm. Repeat with remaining turkey, 1 Tbsp. butter, and 1 Tbsp. oil.

4. Stir wine and next 3 ingredients into skillet, and cook over medium-high heat 2 minutes or until sauce is slightly thickened. Remove from heat; stir in remaining 1 Tbsp. butter. Place turkey on a serving platter; pour sauce over turkey.

* 1 lb. skinned and boned chicken thighs or thin-cut boneless pork chops may be substituted.

sidekick: **SAUTÉED GARLIC SPINACH** Heat 1 Tbsp. olive oil in a Dutch oven over medium heat. Add 3 garlic cloves, thinly sliced, and cook 1 minute or until golden. Add 1 (6-oz.) package fresh baby spinach, and cook 1 minute, turning with tongs. Add another (6-oz.) package fresh baby spinach; cook, turning with tongs, 1 minute or until spinach wilts. Stir in ¼ tsp. salt and ¼ tsp. freshly ground pepper.

savvy secret
from Vanessa:

Pull out your largest nonstick skillet for this recipe. (An electric one would be great.) Don't crowd the pan, and add each turkey cutlet slowly so temperature will stay hot.

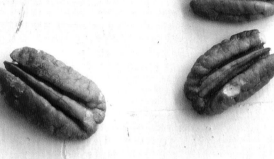

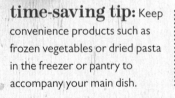

know by heart
Nutty Turkey Cutlets

MAKES 4 SERVINGS
HANDS-ON TIME: 16 MIN.   **TOTAL TIME: 16 MIN.**

¾	cup fine, dry breadcrumbs	½	cup all-purpose flour
½	cup pecans	2	large eggs, lightly beaten
¾	tsp. salt	3	Tbsp. olive oil
¾	tsp. pepper		Garnish: chopped fresh parsley
I	(I-lb.) package turkey cutlets		

1. Process breadcrumbs and pecans in a food processor or blender 10 to 15 seconds or until finely ground.

2. Sprinkle ½ tsp. salt and ½ tsp. pepper over cutlets. Combine flour and remaining salt and pepper in a shallow dish or pie plate. Dredge turkey cutlets in flour mixture; dip in eggs, and dredge in breadcrumb mixture.

3. Sauté cutlets in hot oil in a large skillet over medium-high heat 3 minutes on each side or until golden. Serve immediately. Garnish, if desired.

sidekick: **PARMESAN ANGEL HAIR PASTA** Cook 4 oz. angel hair pasta according to package directions. Drain. Combine cooked pasta, ¼ cup freshly grated Parmesan cheese, and I½ Tbsp. butter; toss well.

time-saving tip: Keep convenience products such as frozen vegetables or dried pasta in the freezer or pantry to accompany your main dish.

healthy

Herb-Blend Turkey Burgers

MAKES 4 SERVINGS
HANDS-ON TIME: 20 MIN.   TOTAL TIME: 20 MIN.

1 lb. lean ground turkey	⅛ tsp. salt
¼ cup chopped fresh basil	4 kaiser rolls, split
2 tsp. lemon zest	Shredded spinach leaves
¾ tsp. minced garlic	Tomato slices

1. Preheat grill to 350° to 400° (medium-high) heat. Stir together first 5 ingredients in a large bowl just until blended. Shape mixture into 4 (5-inch) patties.

2. Grill, covered with grill lid, 5 to 6 minutes on each side or until a meat thermometer inserted into thickest portion registers 170°.

3. Scoop out soft bread from bottom halves of rolls, leaving ¼-inch-thick shells. Place burgers in shells; top with spinach and tomato slices, and cover with roll tops.

sidekick: **PARMESAN FRIES** Preheat oven to 425°. Arrange 1 (26-oz.) package frozen extra-crispy French fried potatoes (we tested with Ore-Ida Extra Crispy Fast Food Fries) in a single layer on 2 lightly greased 15- x 10-inch jelly-roll pans. Place 1 pan on middle oven rack and other on lower oven rack. Bake 15 minutes. Switch pans, and bake 12 to 15 more minutes or until lightly browned. Sprinkle with ¾ tsp. pepper and ½ tsp. kosher salt, tossing lightly. Sprinkle potatoes with ⅔ cup grated Parmesan cheese and ½ tsp. garlic powder. Serve immediately.

Roasted Salmon with Lemon and Dill

MAKES 4 SERVINGS
HANDS-ON TIME: 15 MIN.   **TOTAL TIME: 30 MIN.**

4	(6-oz.) salmon fillets	8	fresh dill sprigs
½	tsp. salt	4	lemon slices, halved
¼	tsp. freshly ground pepper		

1. Preheat oven to 425°. Place salmon fillets on a lightly greased rack in an aluminum foil-lined jelly-roll pan; sprinkle fillets with salt and pepper. Place 2 dill sprigs and 2 lemon slice halves on each fillet.

2. Bake at 425° for 15 to 20 minutes or just until fish flakes with a fork.

sidekick: **BASMATI RICE WITH GREEN PEAS AND FRESH MINT**
Cook 2 (8.5-oz.) pouches ready-to-serve basmati rice according to package directions. Stir in 1 cup frozen sweet peas, thawed; ¼ cup chopped fresh parsley; 1 Tbsp. chopped fresh mint; and salt and pepper to taste.

flavor profile: dill

A symbol of good luck since Roman times, fresh dill lends its sharp flavor and distinct aroma to this fish.

know by heart
Cumin-Dusted Catfish Sandwiches

MAKES 4 SERVINGS
HANDS-ON TIME: 16 MIN.   TOTAL TIME: 16 MIN.

1	cup mayonnaise	2	tsp. ground cumin
3	Tbsp. orange juice	4	(6-oz.) catfish fillets
1	to 2 tsp. minced canned		Vegetable cooking spray
	chipotle chiles in adobo	4	whole wheat hamburger
	sauce		buns, split and toasted
1½	tsp. salt, divided		Tomato slices
¼	cup self-rising cornmeal mix		Lettuce

1. Preheat grill to 350° to 400° (medium-high) heat. Stir together first 3 ingredients and ½ tsp. salt in a small bowl.

2. Combine cornmeal, cumin, and remaining 1 tsp. salt in a shallow bowl. Dredge fillets in cornmeal mixture. Spray fish with cooking spray.

3. Grill fish, covered with grill lid, 3 to 4 minutes on each side or just until fish begins to flake when poked with the tip of a sharp knife and is opaque in center. Serve on buns with mayonnaise mixture, tomato slices, and lettuce.

savvy secret from Vanessa:

Thin fillets of mild, firm-textured fish, such as cod, tilapia, perch, or orange roughy, may be substituted.

sidekick: GRILLED SWEET POTATOES

Coat cold grill cooking grate with cooking spray. Preheat grill to 350° to 400° (medium-high) heat. Pierce 3 medium-size sweet potatoes several times with tines of a fork. Place on a microwave-safe plate; cover with damp paper towels. Microwave at HIGH 6 to 8 minutes or until tender. Let stand 5 minutes. Peel and cut in half lengthwise. Cut into 3 x ½-inch strips. Coat with cooking spray, and sprinkle with ½ tsp. seasoned salt. Place potato strips on grate. Grill potato strips, covered with grill lid, 1 to 2 minutes on each side or until grill marks appear.

Southern-Style Fish Tacos

MAKES 4 SERVINGS
HANDS-ON TIME: 25 MIN.   TOTAL TIME: 25 MIN.

3   large limes, divided
4   (6-oz.) catfish fillets, cut into
      1-inch-thick strips
1½ cups plain yellow cornmeal
2   Tbsp. dried parsley flakes
2   Tbsp. paprika
2   tsp. ground red pepper
2   tsp. lemon pepper
2   tsp. salt
1   tsp. garlic powder
Canola oil

8   (6-inch) fajita-size corn or
      flour tortillas, warmed
1   cup thinly shredded green
      cabbage
1   cup thinly shredded red
      cabbage
1   (16-oz.) container
      refrigerated salsa
Bottled Ranch salad dressing
Toppings: ripe avocado slices,
      diced and seeded tomatoes,
      chopped fresh cilantro

1. Squeeze juice of 1 lime over fish. Combine cornmeal and next 6 ingredients in a large zip-top plastic freezer bag. Pat fish dry with paper towels, and place in bag, shaking to coat.

2. Pour oil to a depth of 1½ inches in a large, deep skillet; heat to 325°. Fry catfish, in batches, in hot oil 2 to 3 minutes or until crispy and golden brown. Drain on paper towels.

3. Place catfish in warm tortillas; top with cabbage, desired amount of salsa, salad dressing, and toppings. Cut remaining 2 limes into wedges, and serve with tacos.

sidekick: **SAUTÉED PINEAPPLE** Melt 1 Tbsp. butter in a large nonstick skillet over medium-high heat. Add 3 cups fresh pineapple chunks, 1 Tbsp. honey, and ½ tsp. curry powder; cook, stirring often, 3 minutes or until thoroughly heated.

no-cook suppers

You don't even have to turn on the oven to make one of these tasty dishes

Pepper Gazpacho

MAKES 8 ¾ CUPS
HANDS-ON TIME: 10 MIN.   TOTAL TIME: 10 MIN.

1 (46-oz.) bottle vegetable juice	1 cup chopped cucumber
1 (12-oz.) jar roasted red bell peppers, drained	½ cup banana pepper rings
1 cup loosely packed fresh parsley leaves	2 garlic cloves
½ cup chopped fresh basil leaves	3 Tbsp. fresh lemon juice
	2 Tbsp. extra virgin olive oil
	Garnishes: sliced cucumber, fresh basil sprig

1. Process half of vegetable juice and next 7 ingredients in a blender until smooth. Transfer to a large bowl. Stir in remaining vegetable juice and 2 Tbsp. olive oil. Serve immediately, or cover and chill up to 2 days. Garnish, if desired.

sidekick: **GREEK SALAD FOCACCIA** Combine 2½ cups mixed salad greens, ½ cup sliced red onion, 3 Tbsp. crumbled reduced-fat feta cheese, 1 Tbsp. fresh lemon juice, 1 Tbsp. extra virgin olive oil, and ⅛ tsp. dried crushed red pepper in a large bowl, tossing well to coat. Cut 1 (6-oz.) focaccia bread in half horizontally. Arrange salad on bottom half of loaf. Replace top half of loaf; cut crosswise into equal portions.

flavor profile: cucumbers

When buying this cool and crisp vegetable, look for those that are dark green and free from blemishes. Avoid those with soft spots or softened ends—both are signs of age. Leave the skin on the cucumbers if you prefer added crunch.

know by heart

Spicy Roasted Red Bell Pepper Pimiento Cheese

MAKES 4 CUPS
HANDS-ON TIME: 20 MIN. **TOTAL TIME: 20 MIN.**

1¼	cups mayonnaise	½	tsp. ground red pepper
½	(12-oz.) jar roasted red bell peppers, drained and chopped	2	(10-oz.) blocks sharp white Cheddar cheese, shredded
2	tsp. finely grated onion		Freshly ground black pepper
2	tsp. coarse-grained mustard		Assorted crackers or apple wedges

1. Stir together mayonnaise and next 4 ingredients until well blended; stir in cheese and freshly ground black pepper to taste. Serve with assorted crackers or apple wedges. Store in an airtight container in refrigerator up to 4 days.

savvy secret
from Vanessa:

A good box-style grater is essential for making the best pimiento cheese. It should give you a choice of hole sizes—a different size on each side. Use the smaller holes for grating hard cheeses, such as Parmesan, and the larger holes for shredding soft cheeses, such as Cheddar.

time-saving tip:

Instead of making your own pimiento cheese, purchase some in the deli of your grocery store. You can dress it up by adding ingredients such as seeded and minced jalapeño peppers, toasted pecans, bacon, olives, or other favorites.

Veggie Rollup

MAKES 4 SERVINGS
HANDS-ON TIME: 8 MINUTES **TOTAL TIME: 23 MINUTES**

4 oz. ⅓-less-fat cream cheese, softened
8 tsp. reduced-fat mayonnaise
½ tsp. fresh dill
½ tsp. chopped fresh parsley
Dash of garlic powder
½ tsp. chopped fresh basil leaves
4 small carrots, diced
4 small celery ribs, diced
4 (8-inch) soft taco-size flour tortillas

1. Stir together first 6 ingredients. Stir in carrots and celery. Spread one-fourth of mixture on I side of each tortilla. Roll up tortillas; wrap with plastic wrap. Chill I5 minutes. Unwrap; cut into I-inch-thick slices.

sidekick: **WATERMELON SALAD** Combine I Tbsp. white balsamic vinegar; 2 tsp. extra virgin olive oil; I tsp. honey; ¼ tsp. freshly ground pepper; and I shallot, minced, in a large bowl. Add 4 cups loosely packed baby arugula and 2 cups cubed seedless watermelon; toss gently to coat. Divide among 4 plates. Sprinkle each serving with I Tbsp. crumbled feta cheese.

table talk: Let everyone in the family "invite" someone famous to dinner tonight by dressing up as a notable person who interests them. Encourage each family member to research their famous person to share a little bit of information about him or her and why that person is appealing. Make a fun game out of guessing who everyone's character is.

Open-Faced Avocado Sandwiches

MAKES 4 SERVINGS
HANDS-ON TIME: 10 MINUTES **TOTAL TIME: 10 MINUTES**

1	avocado, thinly sliced
¼	cup bottled Italian dressing
1	Tbsp. mayonnaise
4	oatmeal or whole wheat bread slices, toasted
1	cup shredded iceberg lettuce
4	(1-oz.) Cheddar cheese slices, halved
4	thin tomato slices

1. Toss avocado slices gently with Italian dressing; drain avocado well, reserving dressing.

2. Spread mayonnaise on 1 side of each bread slice. Top bread slices with lettuce, cheese slices, tomato slices, and avocado.

3. Drizzle sandwiches with reserved Italian dressing, and serve immediately.

sidekick: **MACADAMIA HUMMUS** With food processor running, drop 2 garlic cloves through food chute. Process until minced. Add ½ cup salted macadamia nuts; 3 Tbsp. water; 2 Tbsp. fresh lemon juice; 1 Tbsp. olive oil; and 1 (16-oz.) can chickpeas, drained. Process 1 minute or until smooth. Serve with carrots.

savvy secret *from Vanessa:*

For crisp iceberg lettuce, discard the outer leaves, and core and rinse the lettuce as soon as you get home from the supermarket. Whirl it in a salad spinner, and wrap in paper towels. Place in a zip-top plastic freezer bag, and chill 1 hour or up to 3 days.

savvy secret
from Vanessa:

Cucumber has a mild flavor and crunchy texture, making it a nice addition to salads. When purchasing cucumbers, remember that the smaller the cucumber, the smaller the seeds and the better the flavor. To seed a cucumber, simply cut in half lengthwise, and scrape out the seeds with a spoon.

for company

Tex-Mex Beef-and-Beans Chopped Salad

MAKES 6 SERVINGS
HANDS-ON TIME: 25 MIN.   **TOTAL TIME: 25 MIN.**

¾ cup bottled Ranch dressing
¾ cup refrigerated salsa
2 (10-oz.) packages hearts of romaine lettuce, chopped
1 (15-oz.) can black beans, drained and rinsed
3 cups coarsely crushed tortilla chips
6 oz. pepper Jack cheese, cut into small cubes
1 cup seeded and chopped cucumber
1 cup diced jicama
3 plum tomatoes, chopped
1 medium avocado, chopped
¾ lb. sliced barbecued beef brisket (without sauce), warmed

1. Stir together first 2 ingredients in a small bowl.

2. Toss together romaine and next 7 ingredients. Drizzle with dressing mixture, and top with brisket. Serve immediately.

flavor profile: refrigerated salsa

Find refrigerated salsa in your grocer's produce or deli area. We prefer it in this recipe for its chunky texture and fresh flavor.

kid favorite

Roast Beef Subs

MAKES 4 SERVINGS
HANDS-ON TIME: 15 MIN.   **TOTAL TIME: 15 MIN.**

½ cup (2 oz.) shredded Cheddar cheese	4 (6½-inch) hoagie rolls
⅓ cup diced red bell pepper	4 red leaf lettuce leaves
¼ cup diced red onion	8 (¼-inch-thick) tomato slices
¼ cup bottled Caesar dressing	8 (1-oz.) lean cooked roast beef slices

1. Combine first 4 ingredients in a medium bowl.

2. Cut a ¼-inch-thick slice off top of each roll; set tops aside. Hollow out centers of rolls, leaving ½-inch-thick shells. (Reserve inside of rolls for another use, if desired.) Place 1 lettuce leaf in bottom portion of each roll. Spoon cheese mixture over lettuce; top each serving with 2 tomato slices and 2 slices roast beef. Cover with roll tops.

sidekick: **CARROT SLAW** Combine 4 tsp. rice wine vinegar; 2 tsp. grated fresh ginger; 2 tsp. olive oil; ½ tsp. salt; ½ tsp. freshly ground pepper; and 4 garlic cloves, minced, in a medium bowl. Add 2 cups matchstick carrots, ½ cup shredded radishes, and 2 Tbsp. chopped fresh cilantro; toss to coat.

time-saving tip: The fastest and easiest way to dice a pepper is to first slice it into quarters. Discard the stem and seeds. Slice each quarter into strips; dice the strips.

Peanutty Coleslaw with Shredded Smoked Pork

MAKES 6 SERVINGS
HANDS-ON TIME: 15 MIN.   **TOTAL TIME: 1 HR., 15 MIN.**

½ cup chopped fresh cilantro	1 tsp. grated fresh ginger
¼ cup chopped green onions	½ tsp. salt
3 Tbsp. white vinegar	½ tsp. pepper
1 Tbsp. sesame oil	1 (16-oz.) package shredded
2 Tbsp. mayonnaise	coleslaw mix
2 tsp. wasabi paste	¾ lb. shredded smoked pork
1 tsp. sugar	¾ cup lightly salted peanuts

1. Whisk together first 10 ingredients in a large bowl; add coleslaw mix and pork, stirring to coat. Cover and chill 1 hour; stir in peanuts just before serving.

flavor profile: wasabi paste

Known as a Japanese horseradish, this condiment has an extremely strong flavor and can be purchased in the Asian section of most supermarkets.

savvy secret
from Vanessa:

Your choice of chopped mixed fresh vegetables adds a rainbow of color to this hearty salad. Any combination, such as tomato, radish, celery, broccoli, and carrot, showers it with lots of flavors.

Chef's Salad

MAKES 6 SERVINGS
HANDS-ON TIME: 10 MIN.   TOTAL TIME: 10 MIN.

8	cups mixed salad greens	1	large avocado, sliced
2	cups chopped mixed fresh vegetables	6	cooked bacon slices, crumbled
½	small red onion, cut in half and thinly sliced	3	cups large-cut croutons
3	cups coarsely chopped cooked chicken		Bottled refrigerated Ranch dressing

1. Toss together first 3 ingredients. Top with chicken and avocado; sprinkle with bacon and croutons. Serve with dressing.

sidekick: **BALSAMIC BERRIES** Combine 1 cup quartered small strawberries, 1 cup blueberries, 1 cup raspberries, and 1 Tbsp. bottled balsamic glaze in a bowl; let stand 5 minutes. Spoon berry mixture into small bowls. Top with sour cream.

know by heart

Black Bean 'n' Bacon Wraps

MAKES 4 SERVINGS
HANDS-ON TIME: 10 MIN.   TOTAL TIME: 20 MIN.

½ (8-oz.) package cream cheese, softened

1 Tbsp. taco sauce

4 (6-inch) fajita-size flour tortillas

1 cup canned black beans, drained and rinsed

½ small green bell pepper, diced

3 cooked bacon slices, crumbled

¼ cup (1 oz.) shredded Cheddar cheese

1. Stir together first 2 ingredients; spread mixture on 1 side of each tortilla. Top with black beans and remaining ingredients.

2. Roll tortillas tightly. Wrap in plastic wrap, and chill 10 minutes.

sidekick: **CARROT SALAD** Combine 2 cups matchstick carrots, ½ cup diced red onion, 4 Tbsp. light red wine vinaigrette, and ½ tsp. freshly ground pepper in a medium bowl; toss gently.

flavor profile: Cheddar cheese

The salty tang of Cheddar cheese can range from mild to sharp, making it versatile for both cooking and snacking. It can be white or dyed orange; both deliver a robust quality that can stand alone or be incorporated into soups, casseroles, and sandwiches.

for company

Honey-Chicken Salad

MAKES 4 TO 6 SERVINGS
HANDS-ON TIME: 20 MIN.   TOTAL TIME: 20 MIN.

½	cup chopped pecans	1½	cups mayonnaise
4	cups chopped cooked	⅓	cup honey
	chicken	¼	tsp. salt
3	celery ribs, diced	¼	tsp. pepper
	(about 1½ cups)		Garnish: toasted chopped
¾	cup chopped fresh peaches		pecans
¾	cup fresh blackberries		

1. Combine first 5 ingredients in a large bowl.

2. Whisk together mayonnaise and next 3 ingredients. Add to chicken mixture, stirring gently until combined. Garnish, if desired.

flavor profile: honey

This rich, golden liquid is a natural sweetener that can enhance a variety of dishes. The color and flavor of honey depend on the type of flowers the bees collect the nectar from, but in general, lighter colored honeys have a milder flavor than darker ones. Look for local honey in the summer and fall when it has just been harvested.

sidekick: **GREEN SALAD WITH RASPBERRY VINAIGRETTE**
Process ⅓ cup raspberry or red wine vinegar, ¼ cup sugar, 2 tsp. Dijon mustard, I garlic clove, ½ tsp. salt, and ½ tsp. freshly ground pepper in a blender or food processor until smooth. With blender or processor running, add ½ cup oil in a slow, steady stream; process until smooth. Stir in ¼ cup fresh basil. Top salad greens with sliced vine-ripened tomatoes, cucumbers, and ¼ cup red onion; drizzle with dressing.

healthy

Greek Chicken Salad

MAKES 8 SERVINGS
HANDS-ON TIME: 20 MIN.   TOTAL TIME: 20 MIN.

2	heads romaine lettuce, torn
2	medium tomatoes, chopped
1	large cucumber, chopped
¼	cup chopped fresh parsley
¼	cup chopped green onions
1	tsp. chopped fresh mint
3	cups chopped cooked chicken
4	oz. crumbled feta cheese
½	cup pitted kalamata or black olives, coarsely chopped
1	cup bottled Greek salad dressing

1. Combine first 6 ingredients in a large bowl, tossing gently; top with chicken and next 2 ingredients. Drizzle with desired amount of Greek salad dressing.

flavor profile: parsley

This versatile herb can go in just about every savory dish you cook because its mild, grassy flavor allows the flavors of other ingredients to come through. Curly parsley is less assertive than its brother, flat-leaf parsley (often called Italian parsley). Reach for either when a dish needs a little burst of color.

table talk: American families celebrate this country's Independence Day on July 4th, and many even celebrate Cinco de Mayo on May 5. Add a new tradition by celebrating Greek Independence Day, also known as National Day, on March 25. Family members can dress in blue, the color of the Greek flag, and decorate the table in blue. Have everyone research their favorite Greek island and explain to the table what makes each location special.

savvy secret
from Vanessa:

Red bell peppers are naturally sweet and roasting them adds a smoky savory accent. You can buy jarred roasted red bell peppers at the supermarket, or you can roast your own.

kid favorite

Gouda Chicken Sandwiches

MAKES 4 SERVINGS
HANDS-ON TIME: 18 MIN.   TOTAL TIME: 18 MIN.

4 hoagie rolls	1 (7-oz.) jar roasted red
¼ cup mustard-mayonnaise	bell peppers, drained and
blend	thinly sliced
12 (1-oz.) Gouda cheese slices	8 tomato slices
3 cups cooked chicken, sliced	4 green leaf lettuce leaves

1. Split rolls horizontally; spread with mustard-mayonnaise blend. Top each roll bottom with 3 cheese slices, desired amount of chicken, roasted red pepper slices, tomato slices, and 1 lettuce leaf. Cover with top halves of rolls. Serve immediately.

Note: A whole deli-roasted chicken (about 2½ lb.) will give you just the right amount of meat.

sidekick: **WATERMELON COOLER** Process 4 cups seeded watermelon cubes, ⅓ cup apple juice, 2 Tbsp. fresh lime juice, 1 tsp. chopped fresh mint, ¼ to ½ tsp. ground ginger, and, if desired, 1 Tbsp. honey in a blender or food processor until smooth, stopping to scrape down sides. Cover and chill 1 hour. Garnish with lime wedges and fresh mint sprigs.

Mango-Chicken Pita Sandwiches

MAKES 8 SERVINGS
HANDS-ON TIME: 10 MIN.   TOTAL TIME: 10 MIN.

1	(9-oz.) jar mango chutney	2	cups chopped cooked
½	cup plain yogurt		chicken
1	tsp. lemon zest	8	green leaf lettuce leaves
½	tsp. dry mustard	4	pita bread rounds, halved
1	(10-oz.) package finely		
	shredded cabbage		

1. Combine first 4 ingredients in a large bowl. Stir in cabbage and chicken. Place lettuce leaf in each pita round half. Top with chicken mixture.

sidekick: **APPLE SALAD** Combine 4 large Granny Smith apples, chopped; ½ cup sweetened dried cranberries; ⅓ cup light mayonnaise; 2 Tbsp. fresh lemon juice; and ⅛ tsp. salt in a medium bowl; sprinkle with 5 Tbsp. toasted chopped walnuts. Cover and chill until ready to serve.

savvy secret *from Vanessa:*

Look for mango chutney in the condiment section of your supermarket. Pick up an extra jar to have on hand. Chutney can also be served with chicken or fish entrées or over a block of cream cheese as an appetizer.

kid favorite
Smoked Turkey Wrap

MAKES 1 WRAP
HANDS-ON TIME: 5 MIN.   TOTAL TIME: 5 MIN.

2	Tbsp. whipped cream cheese with chives	4	tomato slices
1	(9-inch) tomato-basil or spinach wrap	1	cup chopped fresh baby spinach
1	Tbsp. Dijon mustard	2	(1-oz.) Cheddar cheese slices
5	(1-oz.) smoked turkey breast slices	1	to 2 Tbsp. chopped fresh basil

1. Spread cream cheese on half of 1 side of wrap. Spread mustard over cream cheese and remaining half of wrap. Top with turkey and remaining ingredients; roll up tightly. Cut in half.

sidekick: **BROCCOLI SLAW** Whisk together ¼ cup light sweet Vidalia onion bottled dressing and 2 tsp. cider vinegar in a large bowl. Add 3 cups fresh broccoli slaw, 1 cup chopped Gala apple, and ¼ cup dried cranberries; toss well to coat.

table talk: Making sandwiches for supper provides the perfect opportunity for a backyard picnic. Pack a basket, grab a blanket, and head to a cozy spot. Take the time to look at the clouds and talk about their different shapes, or discuss other nature discoveries.

Watermelon, Greens, and Pecan Salad

MAKES 6 TO 8 SERVINGS
HANDS-ON TIME: 25 MIN.
TOTAL TIME: 35 MIN., INCLUDING VINAIGRETTE

5 cups seeded and cubed watermelon

1 (6-oz.) package mixed salad greens

Pepper Jelly Vinaigrette

1 cup coarsely chopped smoked chicken

½ cup crumbled Gorgonzola cheese

¾ cup toasted pecan halves

1. Combine watermelon and salad greens in a large bowl; add vinaigrette, tossing gently to coat.

2. Transfer watermelon mixture to a serving platter, and toss with chicken, cheese, and pecans.

Note: We tested with mâche salad greens. This tender heirloom variety of lamb's lettuce has a slightly sweet, nutty flavor and mixes well with baby lettuces.

pepper jelly vinaigrette

MAKES ¾ CUP
HANDS-ON TIME: 5 MIN.   TOTAL TIME: 5 MIN.

¼ cup rice wine vinegar

¼ cup pepper jelly

1 Tbsp. fresh lime juice

1 Tbsp. grated onion

1 tsp. salt

¼ tsp. pepper

¼ cup vegetable oil

1. Whisk together first 6 ingredients in a small bowl. Gradually add oil in a slow, steady stream, whisking until blended.

Turkey, Bacon, and Havarti Sandwich

MAKES 4 SERVINGS
HANDS-ON TIME: 15 MIN.   TOTAL TIME: 1 HR., 15 MIN.

1 (7-inch) round sourdough bread loaf	6 (1-oz.) Havarti cheese slices
¼ cup bottled balsamic vinaigrette	1 (12-oz.) jar roasted red bell peppers, drained and sliced
½ lb. thin smoked deli turkey slices	4 fully cooked bacon slices

1. Cut top 2 inches off sourdough loaf, reserving top; hollow out loaf, leaving a ½-inch-thick shell. (Reserve center of bread loaf for other uses, if desired.)

2. Drizzle 2 Tbsp. vinaigrette in bottom bread shell; layer with half each of turkey, cheese, and peppers. Repeat layers with remaining turkey, cheese, and peppers, and top with bacon. Drizzle with remaining 2 Tbsp. vinaigrette, and cover with reserved bread top; press down firmly.

3. Wrap in plastic wrap, and chill 1 to 8 hours. Cut into 4 wedges.

sidekick: **HONEYED CARROTS** Combine 1 (16-oz.) package baby carrots, 2 Tbsp. honey, 1 Tbsp. butter, 2 tsp. lemon juice, and ¼ tsp. salt in a medium-size microwave-safe dish. Cover and microwave at HIGH 8 to 10 minutes or until tender, stirring after 4 minutes.

flavor profile: Havarti cheese

A semisoft Danish cheese with small irregular holes, Havarti cheese boasts a mild flavor.

healthy

White Bean-and-Tuna Salad

MAKES 3 SERVINGS
HANDS-ON TIME: 6 MIN.   TOTAL TIME: 6 MIN.

time-saving tip:
Don't worry about stemming parsley; its stems are tender and can be chopped and used with the leaves. Simply place the bunch on a cutting board, and chop with a sharp knife.

2	Tbsp. lemon juice
1	Tbsp. olive oil
¼	tsp. salt
½	tsp. freshly ground pepper
½	tsp. dried oregano
1	(20-oz.) can cannellini beans, drained and rinsed
1	(6½-oz.) can solid white tuna in spring water, drained and flaked
4	green onions, thinly sliced
2	Tbsp. chopped fresh parsley
	Lettuce leaves

1. Stir together first 5 ingredients. Add beans and next 2 ingredients, tossing gently to coat. Sprinkle with parsley, and serve over lettuce.

Mediterranean Tuna Salad

MAKES 4 SERVINGS
HANDS-ON TIME: 15 MIN.   TOTAL TIME: 2 HR., 15 MIN.

1 (11-oz.) aluminum foil pouch light tuna chunks in water	2 tsp. lemon zest
1 (15-oz.) can chickpeas, drained and rinsed	1 to 2 Tbsp. fresh lemon juice
⅓ cup chopped pitted kalamata olives	1 tsp. minced garlic
¼ cup olive oil	1 tsp. Dijon mustard
1 shallot, finely chopped	½ tsp. salt
1 Tbsp. drained capers, chopped	½ tsp. pepper
	Assorted torn flatbread or pita
	Arugula
	Feta cheese

1. Stir together first 12 ingredients in a large bowl. Cover and chill 2 to 3 hours. Serve with flatbread, arugula, and feta cheese.

Note: We tested wtih StarKist Flavor Fresh Pouch Chunk Light Tuna In Water.

flavor profile: pouch tuna

This tuna makes a good pantry staple. It's firmer and fresher because it doesn't go through the long canning process.

for company

Crab Salad

MAKES 4 SERVINGS
HANDS-ON TIME: 10 MIN.   **TOTAL TIME: 3 HR., 10 MIN.**

⅓	cup vegetable oil		Arugula
¼	cup cider vinegar	3	medium tomatoes, sliced
½	tsp. salt	3	hard-cooked eggs, peeled
½	tsp. pepper		and quartered
¼	tsp. Worcestershire sauce	12	pitted black olives
1	lb. fresh lump crabmeat,		(optional)
	drained	12	pimiento-stuffed Spanish
1	medium onion, diced		olives (optional)

1. Whisk together first 5 ingredients and ½ cup water. Add crabmeat and onion, tossing gently to coat. Cover and chill 3 hours. Drain.

2. Place desired amount of arugula on serving plates; add tomato slices and crabmeat mixture. Arrange eggs, and, if desired, olives around crabmeat mixture.

table talk: A seafood meal provides the perfect opportunity to have an under-the-sea-themed family supper. The activities can depend on the ages of your children. Younger children might like to dress up like mermaids or other sea creatures. Older children might prefer a family game of Go Fish. Pull out old photos from beach trips to recall fond memories. Let children use their imaginations to decorate the table.

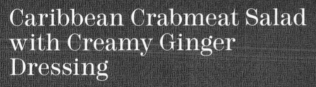

Caribbean Crabmeat Salad with Creamy Ginger Dressing

MAKES 8 SERVINGS
HANDS-ON TIME: 10 MIN.   **TOTAL TIME: 1 HR., 10 MIN.**

1 cup mayonnaise	1 cup diced seedless
1 Tbsp. Dijon mustard	cucumber
1 Tbsp. dry white wine	½ tsp. Old Bay seasoning
1 tsp. ground ginger	¼ tsp. ground white pepper
¼ tsp. salt	Gourmet mixed salad greens
Pinch of sugar	Garnishes: avocado slices, red
1 lb. fresh lump crabmeat	onion rings, mango slices
8 plum tomatoes, diced	

1. Whisk together first 6 ingredients, and chill 1 to 2 hours.

2. Combine crabmeat and next 4 ingredients in a large bowl.
Toss with mayonnaise mixture. Place desired amount of greens
on serving plates; top with crabmeat mixture. Garnish, if desired.

flavor profile: ginger

A warm, slightly woody flavor makes this one of the world's favorite
spices. Ginger gives subtle sweetness to many dishes.

for company

Make-Ahead Shrimp Salad

MAKES 4 TO 6 SERVINGS
HANDS-ON TIME: 12 MIN. TOTAL TIME: 2 HR., 12 MIN.

½   cup mayonnaise
½   cup finely chopped celery
¼   cup finely chopped red onion
2   tsp. Dijon mustard
2   tsp. fresh lemon juice
¼   cup chopped fresh dill
1   tsp. Worcestershire sauce
½   tsp. garlic powder
½   tsp. freshly ground black
     pepper

1   (16-oz.) package frozen
     peeled and deveined
     cooked medium-size shrimp
     (41/50 count)
1   cup grape tomatoes, halved
1   head iceberg lettuce, cut
     into wedges
Garnish: fresh dill sprigs

time-saving tip:
Get a jump start with this easy make-ahead dish—stir it together in the morning, and let it chill until you are ready to serve it for dinner.

1. Combine first 9 ingredients in a large bowl; stir in shrimp and tomatoes. Cover and chill 2 to 12 hours. Serve over lettuce. Garnish, if desired.

slow cooker

*Creating meals on your own
time becomes a snap when you
use this handy appliance*

Slow-Cooker Veggie Chili

MAKES 15 SERVINGS
HANDS-ON TIME: 10 MIN.   **TOTAL TIME: 8 HR., 25 MIN.**

2	large carrots, diced (1 cup)	1	Tbsp. chili powder
2	celery ribs, diced (½ cup)	1	tsp. dried basil
1	medium-size sweet onion, diced	1	tsp. seasoned pepper
2	(8-oz.) packages sliced fresh mushrooms	1	(8-oz.) can tomato sauce
		3	cups tomato juice
1	large zucchini, chopped (1½ cups)	2	(14½-oz.) cans diced tomatoes
1	yellow squash, chopped (1 cup)	4	(15-oz.) cans pinto, black, great Northern, or kidney beans, drained and rinsed
		1	cup frozen whole kernel corn

1. Stir together all ingredients in a 6-qt. slow cooker. Cover and cook on LOW 8 hours.

time-saving tip:

Cool leftovers to room temperature (1 hour), and freeze in plastic freezer containers or zip-top plastic freezer bags for up to 2 months.

sidekick: **VEGGIE QUESADILLAS** Preheat oven to 400°. Coat 1 side of each of 8 (6-inch) fajita-size flour tortillas with vegetable cooking spray. Place tortillas, coated side down, on a baking sheet. Sprinkle each tortilla with 4 Tbsp. shredded Monterey Jack cheese, 4 Tbsp. chopped jarred roasted red bell peppers, 2 Tbsp. chopped fresh cilantro, and 4 tsp. sliced green onions. Fold each tortilla in half. Bake 5 minutes or until cheese is melted. Cut into wedges.

time-saving tip:

Whisking together the tomato paste with the beef broth ensures that there are no lumps of tomato paste in the stew. You can also substitute 2 (1-lb.) packages frozen stew vegetables, thawed, for carrots and potatoes.

for company

Slow-Cooker Beef Stew

MAKES 8 SERVINGS
HANDS-ON TIME: 20 MIN.   **TOTAL TIME: 7 HR., 50 MIN.**

1	(6-oz.) can tomato paste	1	red bell pepper, diced*
¾	cup beef broth	1	(14½-oz.) can diced tomatoes*
2	lb. round steak, cut into 1-inch pieces	⅓	cup red wine
1	lb. carrots, cut into 1-inch pieces	¼	cup all-purpose flour
1	lb. small red potatoes, quartered	2	garlic cloves, minced
1	(8-oz.) package sliced fresh mushrooms	1½	tsp. salt
		1	tsp. pepper
		½	tsp. dried thyme

Garnishes: fresh thyme, freshly ground black pepper

1. Whisk together tomato paste and beef broth in a small bowl. Combine broth mixture, round steak, and next 11 ingredients in a 6-qt. slow cooker. Cover and cook on LOW 7 hours and 30 minutes. Garnish, if desired, just before serving.

* 1 (14½-oz.) can diced tomatoes with green peppers and onions may be substituted for red bell pepper and diced tomatoes.

sidekick: **CHEESY GARLIC BREAD** Preheat broiler with oven rack 5 inches from heat. Cut 2 (6-oz.) French bread baguettes in half lengthwise. Spread 1 garlic clove, pressed, on cut sides of bread; brush with 3 Tbsp. olive oil vinaigrette. Top with 1 tsp. chopped fresh rosemary and ½ cup finely grated Asiago cheese. Broil 4 minutes or until cheese melts and bread is lightly browned. Cut into 16 pieces.

for company

Spicy Steak-and-Black Bean Chili

MAKES 8 SERVINGS
HANDS-ON TIME: 19 MIN.   TOTAL TIME: 8 HR., 19 MIN.

2   lb. boneless top sirloin steak, cubed*
2   Tbsp. vegetable oil
3   (15½-oz.) cans black beans
2   (14½-oz.) cans diced tomatoes
2   (4½-oz.) cans chopped green chiles
1   large sweet onion, diced
1   green bell pepper, diced
4   garlic cloves, minced
1   (12-oz.) can beer
1   (3.625-oz.) package chili seasoning kit
Toppings: shredded Cheddar cheese, diced tomatoes and avocado, sour cream, sliced green onions, chopped fresh cilantro

1. Sauté steak in hot oil in a large skillet over medium-high heat 4 to 5 minutes or until browned.

2. Place steak in a lightly greased 6-qt. slow cooker; stir in black beans and next 6 ingredients. Stir in packets from chili kit, omitting masa and red pepper packets. Cover and cook on LOW 8 hours. Serve with desired toppings.

* 2 lb. ground round may be substituted. Omit oil. Brown ground round in a large skillet over medium-high heat, stirring often, 8 minutes or until meat crumbles and is no longer pink; drain. Proceed with recipe as directed.

Note: We tested with Wick Fowler's 2-Alarm Chili Kit at one tasting and with 1 (4-oz.) package Carroll Shelby's Original Texas Brand Chili Kit at another.

sidekick: **CORNBREAD WAFFLES** Prepare batter from 2 (6-oz.) packages buttermilk cornbread mix according to package directions. Cook batter, in batches, in a preheated, oiled waffle iron until done.

savvy secret
from Vanessa:

A snug-fitting, see-through lid works best on a slow cooker. Removing the cooker's lid during cooking releases a great deal of heat, so you want to be able to see your food through the lid rather than lifting it.

know by heart
Slow-Cooker Roast and Gravy

MAKES 6 SERVINGS
HANDS-ON TIME: 20 MIN.   TOTAL TIME: 8 HR., 20 MIN.

1	(10 ¾-oz.) can cream of mushroom with roasted garlic soup	¼	cup all-purpose flour
1	(10 ½-oz.) can condensed beef broth	1	(3 ½- to 4-lb.) eye-of-round roast, trimmed
1	(1-oz.) envelope dry onion-mushroom soup mix	2	Tbsp. all-purpose flour
		1	tsp. salt
		½	tsp. pepper
		2	Tbsp. vegetable oil

1. Stir together first 3 ingredients and ¼ cup flour until smooth in a 5½-qt. slow cooker.

2. Sprinkle roast with 2 Tbsp. flour, 1 tsp. salt, and ½ tsp. pepper. Brown roast on all sides in hot oil in a large Dutch oven over medium-high heat. Transfer roast to slow cooker.

3. Cover and cook on LOW 8 hours.

4. Remove roast from slow cooker; slice or shred to serve. Skim fat from gravy in slow cooker, if desired. Whisk gravy; serve over roast.

sidekick: **PARMESAN MASHED POTATOES** Prepare 1 (24-oz.) package refrigerated mashed potatoes according to package directions. Stir in ¼ cup freshly grated Parmesan cheese, 2 Tbsp. chopped fresh chives, and ½ tsp. freshly ground pepper. Note: We tested with Simply Potatoes Traditional Mashed Potatoes.

savvy secret
from Vanessa:

Slow cooking requires little fat. Trim excess fat and skin from meats and poultry.

for company

Italian Pot Roast

MAKES 6 SERVINGS
HANDS-ON TIME: 18 MIN.   TOTAL TIME: 8 HR., 58 MIN.

1 (8-oz.) package sliced fresh mushrooms	1 (1-oz.) envelope dry onion soup mix
1 large sweet onion, cut in half and sliced	1 (14-oz.) can beef broth
1 (3- to 4-lb.) boneless chuck roast, trimmed	1 (8-oz.) can tomato sauce
	3 Tbsp. tomato paste
1 tsp. pepper	1 tsp. dried Italian seasoning
2 Tbsp. olive oil	2 Tbsp. cornstarch

1. Place mushrooms and onion in a lightly greased 5- to 6-qt. slow cooker.

2. Sprinkle roast with pepper. Brown roast in hot oil in a large skillet over medium-high heat 2 to 3 minutes on each side.

3. Place roast on top of mushrooms and onion in slow cooker. Sprinkle onion soup mix over roast; pour beef broth and tomato sauce over roast. Cover and cook on LOW 8 to 10 hours or until meat shreds easily with a fork.

4. Transfer roast to a cutting board; cut into large chunks, removing any large pieces of fat. Keep roast warm.

5. Skim fat from juices in slow cooker; stir in tomato paste and Italian seasoning. Stir together cornstarch and 2 Tbsp. water in a small bowl until smooth; add to juices in slow cooker, stirring until blended. Increase slow cooker heat to HIGH. Cover and cook 40 minutes or until mixture is thickened. Stir in roast.

sidekick: **TORTELLINI PRIMAVERA** Sauté 2 cups diced zucchini, 1 cup frozen sweet peas, and ½ cup diced onion in 3 Tbsp. hot olive oil until tender. Toss with 20 oz. hot cooked cheese-and-spinach tortellini and ½ cup each shredded Parmesan cheese and chopped fresh basil leaves. Season with salt and pepper to taste.

flavor profile: olive oil

Regular olive oil is a blend of refined olive oil and extra-virgin olive oil. It costs less and has a mild flavor. Use it when you want to preserve the flavors of the food rather than impart the character of the oil to it. Regular olive oil is often used for sautéing and stir-frying.

Meatloaf

MAKES 6 SERVINGS
HANDS-ON TIME: 15 MIN.   TOTAL TIME: 5 HR., 25 MIN.

sidekick: **SHREDDED RANCH POTATOES** Sauté 1 (30-oz.) package frozen shredded country-style hash browns in a large skillet coated with cooking spray over medium-high heat about 6 minutes or until crispy and cooked through. Stir in ¼ cup each chopped fresh parsley, sour cream, and bottled Ranch dressing. Add 1 tsp. freshly ground pepper and ½ tsp. salt.

2 lb. ground round	1 large egg
1 (1-oz.) envelope dry onion soup mix	1 Tbsp. Worcestershire sauce
1 cup (4 oz.) shredded sharp Cheddar cheese	1 cup ketchup, divided
¾ cup fine, dry breadcrumbs	1 Tbsp. light brown sugar
	1 tsp. yellow mustard

1. Combine first 6 ingredients, ½ cup ketchup, and ¼ cup water; shape mixture into an 8- x 4-inch loaf. Line bottom and sides of a 4-qt. oval-shaped slow cooker with aluminum foil, allowing 2 inches to extend over sides. Lightly grease foil. Place loaf in slow cooker.

2. Stir together brown sugar, mustard, and remaining ½ cup ketchup; spread over top of loaf. Cover and cook on LOW 5 to 6 hours or until a meat thermometer registers 160°. Lift loaf from slow cooker, using foil sides as handles. Let stand 10 minutes before serving.

Note: You may also prepare in a 5-qt. slow cooker. Cover and cook on LOW 3½ hours or until a meat thermometer registers 160°.

Slow-Cooker Barbecue Pork

MAKES 6 SERVINGS
HANDS-ON TIME: 5 MIN.   **TOTAL TIME: 8 HR., 5 MIN.**

savvy secret
from Vanessa:

This pork is one of my favorites for parties—served with slaw on dinner rolls! Serve on small rolls as an appetizer or for your next tailgate. It's also great for an easy dinner after baseball games.

1   (3- to 4-lb.) boneless pork shoulder roast (Boston butt), trimmed

1   (18-oz.) bottle barbecue sauce
1   (12-oz.) can cola soft drink
Garnish: sliced green onions

1. Place roast in a lightly greased 6-qt. slow cooker; pour barbecue sauce and cola over roast. Cover and cook on LOW 8 to 10 hours or until meat shreds easily with a fork.

2. Transfer pork to a cutting board; shred with two forks, removing any large pieces of fat. Skim fat from sauce, and stir in shredded pork. Garnish, if desired

sidekick: **CHEESE GRITS** Bring 2 cups fat-free milk and 1¼ cups water to a boil in a medium saucepan over medium-high heat. Slowly add ¾ cup quick-cooking grits, stirring with a whisk. Cover, reduce heat, and simmer, stirring occasionally, 5 minutes or until thickened. Remove from heat. Add 1 cup shredded reduced-fat sharp Cheddar cheese, 1 Tbsp. butter, ½ tsp. salt, and ⅛ tsp. freshly ground pepper; stir until cheese melts. Serve pork over grits, if desired.

kid favorite

Slow-Cooker Red Beans and Rice

MAKES ABOUT 10 CUPS
HANDS-ON TIME: 15 MIN.   **TOTAL TIME: 7 HR., 15 MIN.**

1	lb. dried red kidney beans	3	garlic cloves, minced
½	lb. andouille smoked chicken	1	Tbsp. Creole seasoning
	sausage, thinly sliced	3	cups uncooked long-grain
3	celery ribs, chopped		rice
1	green bell pepper, chopped		Garnish: sliced green onions
1	medium onion, chopped		

1. Stir together first 7 ingredients and 7 cups water in a 4-qt. slow cooker. Cover and cook on HIGH 7 hours or until beans are tender.

2. Meanwhile, cook rice according to package directions. Serve with red bean mixture. Garnish, if desired.

Note: We tested with Aidells Organic Fully Cooked Cajun Style Andouille Smoked Chicken Sausage.

time-saving tip:

To mince garlic, loosen the papery skin from garlic; place the flat side of a knife on the clove. Press down using the heel of your hand, or lightly tap the knife with your fist to break and loosen the skin. Peel off the papery skin; slice off the tough end with a knife. Make thin, lengthwise cuts through the clove, and then cut the strips crosswise.

sidekick: VINEGAR SLAW

Whisk together 1 Tbsp. sugar, 3 Tbsp. cider vinegar, 2 tsp. vegetable oil, and ¼ tsp. salt in a large bowl until sugar dissolves. Add 1 (16-oz.) package coleslaw mix and ¼ cup chopped green onions to vinegar mixture; toss until well coated. Serve immediately.

for company

King Ranch Chicken

MAKES 6 SERVINGS
HANDS-ON TIME: 10 MIN.   **TOTAL TIME: 4 HR., 10 MIN.**

4	cups chopped cooked chicken	1	(10-oz.) can diced tomatoes and green chiles
1	large onion, chopped	1	garlic clove, minced
1	large green bell pepper, chopped	1	tsp. chili powder
1	(10¾-oz.) can cream of chicken soup	12	(6-inch) fajita-size corn tortillas
1	(10¾-oz.) can cream of mushroom soup	2	cups (8 oz.) shredded sharp Cheddar cheese

1. Stir together first 8 ingredients. Tear tortillas into 1-inch pieces; layer one-third of tortilla pieces in a lightly greased 6-qt. slow cooker. Top with one-third of chicken mixture and ⅔ cup cheese. Repeat layers twice.

2. Cover and cook on LOW 3½ hours or until bubbly and edges are golden brown. Uncover and cook on LOW 30 minutes.

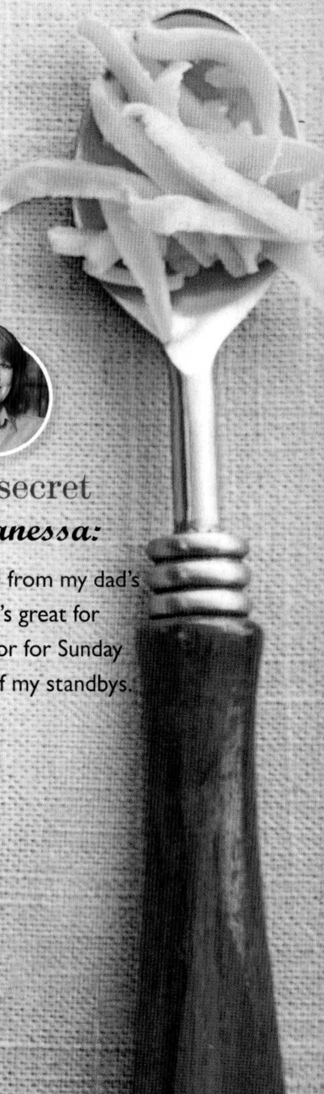

savvy secret
from Vanessa:

This was adapted from my dad's favorite recipe. It's great for church potlucks or for Sunday lunch—it's one of my standbys.

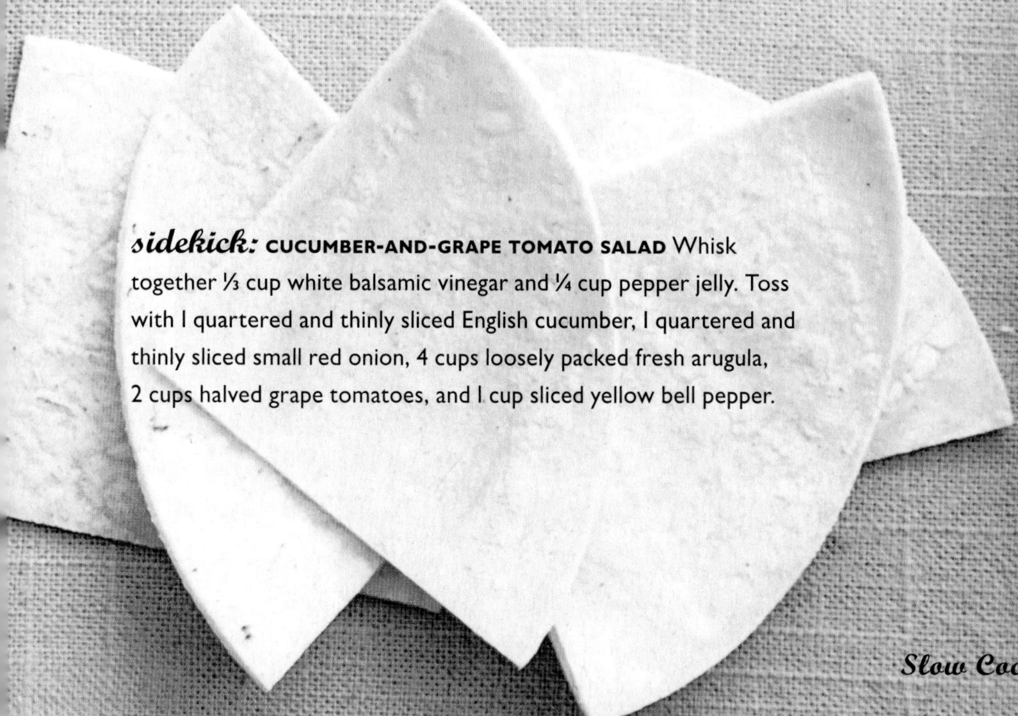

sidekick: **CUCUMBER-AND-GRAPE TOMATO SALAD** Whisk together ⅓ cup white balsamic vinegar and ¼ cup pepper jelly. Toss with 1 quartered and thinly sliced English cucumber, 1 quartered and thinly sliced small red onion, 4 cups loosely packed fresh arugula, 2 cups halved grape tomatoes, and 1 cup sliced yellow bell pepper.

Chicken-and-Spinach Lasagna

MAKES 6 SERVINGS
HANDS-ON TIME: 20 MIN.   TOTAL TIME: 4 HR., 30 MIN.

1 (10-oz.) package frozen chopped spinach, thawed	1 cup chicken broth
3 cups chopped cooked chicken	½ tsp. pepper
2 cups matchstick carrots	4 cups (16 oz.) shredded Italian cheese blend, divided
2 (10-oz.) packages refrigerated Alfredo sauce*	9 uncooked lasagna noodles
1 (10¾-oz.) can cream of mushroom soup**	¼ cup chopped fresh basil

savvy secret from Vanessa:

This is one of my all-time favorite slow-cooker recipes. Your family will love this one—perfect for company or weeknight suppers.

1. Drain spinach well, pressing between paper towels. Stir together spinach, chicken, next 5 ingredients, and 3 cups Italian cheese blend in a large bowl.

2. Spoon one-fourth of chicken mixture into a lightly greased 6-qt. slow cooker. Arrange 3 noodles over chicken mixture, breaking to fit. Repeat layers twice. Top with remaining chicken mixture and 1 cup cheese. Cover and cook on LOW 3½ hours or until noodles are done, mixture is bubbly, and edges are golden brown. Uncover and cook on LOW 30 minutes. Sprinkle with basil. Let stand 10 minutes before serving.

* Reduced-fat Alfredo sauce may be substituted.

** Reduced-fat cream of mushroom soup may be substituted.

sidekick: **GRAPEFRUIT SALAD** Toss 1 (5-oz.) package mixed salad greens with 2 cups each refrigerated red grapefruit sections and sliced avocado, ½ cup sweetened dried cranberries, and ⅓ cup bottled poppy-seed dressing.

Creamy Slow-Cooker Chicken

MAKES 6 SERVINGS
HANDS-ON TIME: 20 MINUTES   **TOTAL TIME: 4 HR., 20 MIN.**

6	skinned and boned chicken breasts (about 2 ½ lb.)	½	cup dry white wine
2	tsp. seasoned salt	1	(0.7-oz.) envelope Italian dressing mix
2	Tbsp. canola oil	1	(8-oz.) package sliced fresh mushrooms
1	(10 ¾-oz.) can reduced-fat cream of mushroom soup		
1	(8-oz.) package ⅓-less-fat cream cheese		

1. Sprinkle chicken with seasoned salt. Cook chicken, in batches, in hot oil in a large skillet over medium-high heat 2 to 3 minutes on each side or just until browned. Transfer chicken to a 5-qt. slow cooker, reserving drippings in skillet. Add soup, cream cheese, white wine, and dressing mix to drippings in skillet. Cook over medium heat, stirring constantly, 2 to 3 minutes or until cheese melts and mixture is smooth.

2. Arrange mushrooms over chicken in slow cooker. Spoon soup mixture over mushrooms. Cover and cook on LOW 4 hours. Stir well just before serving.

time-saving tip:

To make ahead, prepare recipe as directed. Transfer to a 13- x 9-inch baking dish, and let cool completely. Freeze up to 1 month. Thaw in refrigerator 8 to 24 hours. To reheat, cover tightly with aluminum foil, and bake at 325° for 45 minutes. Uncover and bake 15 minutes or until thoroughly heated.

for company

Creole Chicken with Field Pea Succotash

MAKES 6 SERVINGS
HANDS-ON TIME: 10 MIN.   TOTAL TIME: 5 HR., 10 MIN.

1 (16-oz.) package frozen field peas with snaps, thawed	2 tsp. chicken bouillon granules
1 (10-oz.) package frozen vegetable gumbo mix, thawed	4 tsp. Creole seasoning, divided
	1½ tsp. paprika
1 (16-oz.) package frozen baby gold and white whole kernel corn, thawed	6 skinned, bone-in chicken thighs (about 2½ lb.)

1. Stir together first 4 ingredients and 2 tsp. Creole seasoning in a lightly greased 6-qt. oval-shaped slow cooker.

2. Combine paprika and remaining 2 tsp. Creole seasoning; rub over chicken. Arrange chicken on top of vegetable mixture. Cover and cook on LOW 5 to 6 hours or until chicken is done.

sidekick: **VINEGAR TOMATOES** Drizzle sliced fresh tomatoes with bottled oil-and-vinegar dressing; season with salt and pepper to taste.

savvy secret
from Vanessa:

Be sure to use bone-in chicken thighs for this slow-cooker favorite, as this will not work with boneless, skinless chicken thighs.

Chicken Thighs with Carrots and Potatoes

MAKES 6 SERVINGS
HANDS-ON TIME: 20 MIN.   TOTAL TIME: 6 HR., 20 MIN.

1	medium onion	½	tsp. dried thyme
4	medium-size new potatoes (about 1 lb.)	1¼	tsp. salt, divided
2	cups baby carrots	½	tsp. pepper, divided
¼	cup chicken broth	1	tsp. paprika
¼	cup dry white wine	6	skinned, bone-in chicken thighs
1	tsp. minced garlic		Garnish: fresh thyme

1. Halve onion lengthwise, and cut into ¼-inch-thick slices. Cut potatoes into ¼-inch-thick wedges. Place onion in a lightly greased 6-qt. slow cooker; top with potatoes and carrots.

2. Combine broth, next 3 ingredients, ¾ tsp. salt, and ¼ tsp. pepper. Pour over vegetables.

3. Combine paprika and remaining ½ tsp. salt and ¼ tsp. pepper; rub over chicken. Arrange chicken on top of vegetables.

4. Cover and cook on LOW 6 hours or until chicken is done and vegetables are tender. Garnish, if desired.

savvy secret
from Vanessa:

Substitute an extra ¼ cup chicken broth in place of wine, if you prefer.

flavor profile: thyme

This congenial herb pairs well with many other herbs—especially rosemary, parsley, sage, savory, and oregano. Because the leaves are so small, they often don't require chopping. Thyme makes a perfect garnish as well.

Turkey Breast and Herb-Cornbread Stuffing

MAKES 8 SERVINGS
HANDS-ON TIME: 25 MIN.   TOTAL TIME: 5 HR., 30 MIN.

1 (6-oz.) package buttermilk cornbread and muffin mix	½ cup chopped celery
1 (2½-lb.) bone-in, skin-on turkey breast	¼ cup chopped fresh parsley
1 tsp. salt	1½ tsp. poultry seasoning
¼ tsp. pepper	1½ cups herb-seasoned stuffing
¼ cup butter	2 large eggs, lightly beaten
½ cup chopped onion	1 (14-oz.) can low-sodium chicken broth

1. Prepare cornbread mix according to package directions; let cool completely (about 30 minutes). Coarsely crumble cornbread (about 3 cups).

2. Rinse turkey, and pat dry. Sprinkle with salt and pepper.

3. Melt butter in a large skillet over medium heat; add turkey to skillet, skin side down, and cook 3 to 4 minutes or until browned. Remove from skillet. Add onion and next 3 ingredients to skillet, and sauté 3 to 5 minutes or until tender.

4. Stir together onion mixture, stuffing, next 2 ingredients, and crumbled cornbread in a large bowl.

5. Place cornbread stuffing mixture in a lightly greased 6-qt. slow cooker. Top with turkey, skin side up. Cover and cook on LOW 4 hours or until a meat thermometer inserted into thickest portion registers 170° and stuffing registers 165°. Remove turkey from slow cooker, and let stand 15 minutes before serving.

Note: We tested with Martha White Buttermilk Cornbread & Muffin Mix and Pepperidge Farm Herb Seasoned Stuffing.

table talk: Make tonight's dinner a discussion of the "word of the day." Give each family member a word and its meaning with instructions that they must incorporate it into their conversations that day. Let everyone report back at dinner about how he or she used the word. Take turns assigning words.

healthy
Slow-Cooker Turkey Chili

MAKES 4 TO 6 SERVINGS
HANDS-ON TIME: 20 MIN.   TOTAL TIME: 6 HR., 20 MIN.

1 ¼ lb. lean ground turkey
1   large onion, chopped
1   garlic clove, minced
1   (1.25-oz.) envelope chili seasoning mix
1   (12-oz.) can beer
1 ½ cups frozen corn kernels
1   red bell pepper, chopped
1   green bell pepper, chopped

1   (28-oz.) can crushed tomatoes
1   (15-oz.) can black beans, drained and rinsed
1   (8-oz.) can tomato sauce
¾   tsp. salt

Toppings: shredded Cheddar cheese, finely chopped red onion, sliced fresh jalapeño peppers

1. Cook first 4 ingredients in a large skillet over medium-high heat, stirring often, 8 minutes or until turkey crumbles and is no longer pink. Stir in beer, and cook, stirring occasionally, 2 minutes. Spoon mixture into a 5½-qt. slow cooker; stir in corn and next 6 ingredients until well blended. Cover and cook on LOW 6 hours. Serve with desired toppings.

sidekick: **TOMATO-AND-GARLIC CROSTINI** Heat a grill pan over medium-high heat. Add 8 (½-inch-thick) ciabatta slices to pan. Cook 1 minute on each side or until toasted. Halve 4 garlic cloves and 1 medium-size ripe tomato. Rub 1 side of each piece of toasted ciabatta with a garlic half, cut side down, until toast is fragrant. Rub tomato halves over toast slices to release juices onto bread. Drizzle each with ½ tsp olive oil. Sprinkle ¼ tsp. salt over toast slices.

picky eaters

Don't be a short-order cook any longer—create scrumptious meals that the whole family will love

know by heart

Vegetable Melt

MAKES 4 SANDWICHES
HANDS-ON TIME: 30 MIN. **TOTAL TIME: 30 MIN.**

HERB MAYONNAISE

¼	cup mayonnaise
1	Tbsp. chopped fresh parsley
½	tsp. lemon zest
1	Tbsp. fresh lemon juice

SANDWICHES

8	multigrain bread slices
1	(6-oz.) package mozzarella cheese slices
¼	cup finely chopped roasted red bell pepper
½	(14-oz.) can quartered artichoke hearts, drained and chopped
1	cup firmly packed arugula
¼	cup butter, softened

1. Prepare Herb Mayonnaise: Combine first 4 ingredients. Chill until ready to use.

2. Prepare Sandwiches: Spread a thin layer of Herb Mayonnaise on 1 side of each bread slice. Layer 4 bread slices, mayonnaise sides up, each with 1 cheese slice, 1 Tbsp. red bell pepper, 1 rounded tablespoonful artichoke hearts, and ¼ cup arugula. Top with remaining cheese and bread slices, mayonnaise sides down. Spread butter on outside of each sandwich.

3. Cook sandwiches in a large nonstick skillet or griddle over medium-high heat 3 to 4 minutes on each side or until lightly browned and cheese is melted. Serve immediately.

sidekick: **SWEET POTATO FRIES WITH ROSEMARY KETCHUP**
Prepare frozen sweet potato fries as directed. Meanwhile, stir together 1 (14.5-oz.) can fire-roasted diced tomatoes with garlic, drained; ½ cup ketchup; 1 garlic clove, minced; and ½ tsp. dried rosemary. Serve with fries. Note: This dip also works well for french fries, or toss the mixture with refrigerated cooked red potatoes for a quick potato salad.

flavor profile: arugula, also known as rocket

This aromatic, leafy green is a member of the same botanical family as mustard, cabbage, and broccoli. Arugula's flavor is often likened to peppery mustard, making it somewhat stronger than most lettuces, so it's often mixed with other greens. Find it as loose leaves in bins or in bags. Look for firm, fresh, uniformly green leaves without yellow or brown spots.

for company

Sautéed Mushroom-and-Cheese Ravioli

MAKES 4 TO 6 SERVINGS
HANDS-ON TIME: 25 MIN.   **TOTAL TIME: 35 MIN.**

1 (25-oz.) package frozen cheese-filled ravioli	½ tsp. kosher salt
3 Tbsp. butter	½ tsp. pepper
1 Tbsp. olive oil	2 Tbsp. chopped fresh parsley or basil
1 (8-oz.) package sliced fresh mushrooms	3 Tbsp. grated Parmesan cheese
¼ cup finely chopped sweet onion	

1. Cook ravioli according to package directions in a Dutch oven; drain and keep warm. Wipe Dutch oven clean.

2. Melt 2 Tbsp. butter with oil in Dutch oven over medium-high heat; add mushrooms and next 3 ingredients, and sauté 8 to 10 minutes or until vegetables are tender. Reduce heat to low, and stir in ravioli and remaining 1 Tbsp. butter, and cook, stirring often, until butter is melted. Add parsley, and toss gently to combine. Sprinkle with cheese, and serve immediately.

Note: We tested with Rosetto Cheese Ravioli.

savvy secret from Vanessa:

Grow fresh herbs with your children. Let the kids taste them, and stir them into different foods. Older kids can also cut up herbs using kitchen scissors.

kid favorite

Cheesy BBQ Sloppy Joes

MAKES 4 SERVINGS
HANDS-ON TIME: 28 MIN.   TOTAL TIME: 28 MIN.

1½ lb. lean ground beef
1 (14.5-oz.) can diced tomatoes
1 cup ketchup
½ cup bottled barbecue sauce
1 Tbsp. Worcestershire sauce
2 Tbsp. chopped pickled jalapeño peppers (optional)
1 Tbsp. liquid from pickled jalapeño peppers (optional)

1 (11.25-oz.) package frozen garlic Texas toast
½ cup (2 oz.) shredded sharp Cheddar cheese
Pickled jalapeño pepper slices (optional)

1. Brown ground beef in a large skillet over medium-high heat, stirring often, 8 to 10 minutes or until beef crumbles and is no longer pink; drain well. Return to skillet. Stir in tomatoes, next 3 ingredients, and, if desired, jalapeño peppers and liquid. Cover and cook 10 minutes.

2. Meanwhile, prepare Texas toast according to package directions. Serve beef mixture over Texas toast; sprinkle with cheese and, if desired, pepper slices.

sidekick: **ONION-AND-HERB COLESLAW** Whisk together ⅓ cup mayonnaise, ¼ cup buttermilk, 1 tsp. salt-free onion-and-herb seasoning blend, ¼ tsp. salt, and ⅛ tsp. pepper until well blended. Pour mayonnaise mixture over 1 (16-oz.) package shredded coleslaw mix; toss well. Chill until ready to serve.

flavor profile: pickled jalapeño peppers

Growing up in Texas, we ate these as pickles. There are mild and hot varieties. You could substitute sliced pepperoncini salad peppers, which have the same briny flavor but less heat.

know by heart
Taco Pizzas

MAKES 6 SERVINGS
HANDS-ON TIME: 25 MIN.   **TOTAL TIME: 40 MIN.**

1 lb. ground pork*	1½ cups (6 oz.) shredded colby-Jack cheese blend
1 (1.25-oz.) package 40%-less-sodium taco seasoning mix	1 (24-oz.) package prebaked pizza crusts
¼ cup chopped fresh cilantro	1 (16-oz.) can fat-free refried beans
1 (11-oz.) can Mexican-style corn, drained and rinsed	Toppings: shredded lettuce, sour cream
1 (10-oz.) can mild diced tomatoes and green chiles, drained	Garnish: cilantro sprig

1. Preheat oven to 425°. Cook pork in a large skillet over medium-high heat 5 minutes, stirring until meat crumbles and is no longer pink; drain well on paper towels. Wipe out skillet with a paper towel. Return pork to skillet; stir in taco seasoning mix and ⅔ cup water; cook according to package directions on seasoning mix. Remove mixture from heat, and stir in chopped cilantro and next 3 ingredients.

2. Place pizza crusts on baking sheets. Spread beans over crusts, leaving a ¼-inch border around edges. Top beans with pork mixture.

3. Bake, 1 pizza at a time, at 425° for 6 to 8 minutes or until thoroughly heated and cheese melts. Remove from oven, and let stand 5 minutes. Repeat with remaining pizza. Serve with desired toppings. Garnish, if desired.

* 1 lb. ground chuck may be substituted for ground pork.

Note: We tested with Old El Paso 40% Less Sodium Taco Seasoning Mix and Mama Mary's Traditional Gourmet Pizza Crusts.

time-saving tip: This recipe makes 2 (12-inch) pizzas. If your family won't eat both pizzas on the same night, save half the ingredients for the second pizza at another meal.

table talk: Convert a favorite school time ritual into dinner time by making tonight "show and tell," where everyone brings a special item to the table and describes why it is meaningful to them.

for company

Chili-Cheese Bake

MAKES 8 SERVINGS
HANDS-ON TIME: 20 MIN.   TOTAL TIME: 1 HR., 20 MIN.

- 2   lb. lean ground beef
- 1   onion, chopped
- 2   (15½-oz.) cans chili starter
- 1   (14½-oz.) can petite diced tomatoes
- 1   (11-oz.) can whole kernel corn with red and green bell peppers, drained and rinsed
- 1   (8-oz.) package reduced-fat shredded colby-Jack cheese blend
- 1   (32-oz.) package frozen seasoned potato nuggets

1. Preheat oven to 350°. Cook ground beef and onion in a large skillet over medium-high heat, stirring often, 8 to 10 minutes or until meat crumbles and is no longer pink. Drain well, and return meat mixture to skillet. Stir in chili starter and next 2 ingredients.

2. Pour mixture into a lightly greased 13- x 9-inch baking dish. Sprinkle with cheese; top with potato nuggets.

3. Bake at 350° for 1 hour or until potatoes are golden.

Note: We tested with Bush's Chili Magic Chili Starter Traditional Mild and Ore-Ida Tater Tots. To kick up the flavor, substitute 1 (14½-oz.) can petite diced tomatoes and green chiles for petite diced tomatoes.

sidekick: **MIXED GREENS WITH GARLIC OIL DRESSING** Whisk together 2 garlic cloves, minced; 2 tsp. chopped fresh oregano; ½ tsp. freshly ground black pepper; ¼ tsp. salt; 3 Tbsp. fresh lime juice; and 2 Tbsp. water in a large bowl. Whisk in 3 Tbsp. olive oil. Add 2 (5-oz.) packages spring greens mix, and toss gently to coat.

Lasagna Pizza Cups

MAKES 10 PIZZA CUPS
HANDS-ON TIME: 25 MIN.   **TOTAL TIME: 45 MIN.**

½ lb. lean ground beef
½ small onion, chopped
2 garlic cloves, minced
½ (15-oz.) jar pizza sauce, divided

1 (7.5-oz.) can refrigerated buttermilk biscuits
½ cup ricotta cheese
¾ cup (3 oz.) shredded mozzarella cheese

1. Preheat oven to 375°. Cook first 3 ingredients in a large skillet over medium heat, stirring occasionally, 5 minutes or until meat crumbles and is no longer pink. Drain well. Return meat mixture to skillet; stir in 1 cup pizza sauce. Remove from heat.

2. Press biscuits on bottom and up sides of lightly greased muffin cups. Spoon about 1 rounded tablespoonful meat mixture into each biscuit cup; top with ricotta cheese (about 1 heaping teaspoonful each). Sprinkle with shredded mozzarella cheese.

3. Bake at 375° for 18 to 20 minutes or until golden. Remove from oven, and gently run a knife around outer edge of pizza cups to loosen from sides of pan. Remove cups from pan, using a spoon.

4. Place remaining pizza sauce in a small microwave-safe glass bowl; cover with plastic wrap. Microwave at HIGH 10 to 15 seconds or until thoroughly heated. Serve pizza cups with warm sauce.

Note: We tested with Ragú Homemade Style Pizza Sauce.

sidekick: **ROMAINE SALAD** Whisk together ⅓ cup fresh lemon juice; 1 tsp. Worcestershire sauce; 2 garlic cloves, pressed; ¾ tsp. kosher salt; and ½ tsp. freshly ground pepper. Whisk in ½ cup olive oil. Place 1 head romaine lettuce, torn, in a large bowl. Pour olive oil mixture over lettuce, and toss. Sprinkle with ½ cup freshly grated or shredded Parmesan cheese, tossing to combine. Top with 1 cup large plain croutons, and serve immediately.

savvy secret
from Vanessa:

These make a great after-school snack.

Barbecued Pork Quesadillas

MAKES 4 SERVINGS
HANDS-ON TIME: 30 MIN.   TOTAL TIME: 42 MIN.

½	lb. shredded barbecued pork	8	(6-inch) fajita-size flour tortillas
½	cup barbecue sauce	1	cup (4 oz.) shredded Mexican four-cheese blend
¼	cup chopped fresh cilantro		
5	green onions, minced	2	Tbsp. butter, softened

1. Stir together first 4 ingredients.

2. Spoon one-fourth of the pork mixture on 1 side of each tortilla; sprinkle with cheese. Fold tortillas in half, pressing gently to seal. Spread butter on both sides of tortillas.

3. Heat a large nonstick or cast-iron skillet over medium heat, and cook quesadillas 2 to 3 minutes on each side or until browned.

sidekick: **GARLIC-CHILI CORN** Melt a few tablespoons of butter with minced garlic and a dash of chili powder in a microwave-safe bowl; pour over boiled or grilled corn on the cob.

savvy secret from Vanessa:

Quesadillas make quick, delicious weeknight meals. You can add any ingredients you like, but since the cook time in the pan is relatively short, you'll need to cook your filling ingredients first. To best cut quesadillas, place them on a cutting board and cut into wedges using a serrated knife. Keep quesadillas warm in a 200° oven until everyone is seated at the table.

Pineapple Grilled Pork Tenderloin

MAKES 6 SERVINGS
HANDS-ON TIME: 18 MIN.   TOTAL TIME: 48 MIN.

2 (1-lb.) pork tenderloins	¼ cup orange marmalade
1 tsp. salt	3 Tbsp. hoisin sauce
½ tsp. freshly ground pepper	3 Tbsp. soy sauce
1 (8-oz.) can pineapple slices in juice	2 garlic cloves, pressed
1 Tbsp. lime juice	1 tsp. Dijon mustard
1 tsp. lime zest	½ tsp. ground ginger

1. Preheat grill to 350° to 400° (medium-high) heat. Remove silver skin from tenderloins, leaving a thin layer of fat. Sprinkle pork with salt and pepper.

2. Drain pineapple, reserving ⅓ cup juice.

3. Bring lime juice, next 7 ingredients, and reserved pineapple juice to a boil in a saucepan over medium-high heat. Boil 3 to 4 minutes or until slightly thickened. Reserve half of mixture in a bowl.

4. Grill pork, covered with grill lid, 10 to 12 minutes on each side or until a meat thermometer inserted into thickest portion registers 145°, basting with remaining half of pineapple-marmalade mixture. Remove from grill; cover with aluminum foil, and let stand 10 minutes.

5. Meanwhile, grill pineapple slices 1 to 2 minutes on each side. Serve grilled pineapple slices and reserved pineapple-marmalade mixture with grilled pork.

sidekick: **ROASTED SWEET POTATOES** Cube 2 large sweet potatoes (about 2 lb.), and toss with 2 Tbsp. olive oil. Bake at 425° for 25 minutes. Remove from oven, and toss with 1 tsp. salt and ½ tsp. pepper.

table talk: Create a family dinner question box by letting younger kids decorate a shoebox with construction paper, stickers, and cutouts. Cut a slit in the top of the box, and encourage family members to place questions inside the box. Pass the box around the dinner table, and let each member pull out a question and answer it.

Caribbean Pork with Butter Bean Toss

MAKES 4 SERVINGS
HANDS-ON TIME: 15 MIN.   TOTAL TIME: 45 MIN.

1	lb. pork tenderloin	¼ cup chopped fresh parsley
3	Tbsp. olive oil, divided	1 tsp. fresh thyme leaves
1½	tsp. salt, divided	¼ cup fresh lemon juice
1	Tbsp. Caribbean jerk seasoning	1 Tbsp. sugar
3	cups fresh or frozen butter beans	½ tsp. dried crushed red pepper
		¼ tsp. ground black pepper

1. Preheat grill to 350° to 400° (medium-high) heat. Remove silver skin from tenderloin, leaving a thin layer of fat. Rub 1 Tbsp. olive oil, ½ tsp. salt, and 1 Tbsp. Caribbean seasoning over tenderloin.

2. Grill tenderloin, covered with grill lid, 10 to 12 minutes on each side or until a meat thermometer inserted into thickest portion registers 145°. Remove from grill, and let stand 5 minutes before slicing.

3. Meanwhile, bring butter beans and water to cover to a boil in a 3-qt. saucepan over high heat; reduce heat to medium, and simmer 25 minutes. Drain. Combine beans, next 6 ingredients, and remaining 2 Tbsp. olive oil and 1 tsp. salt. Serve with sliced pork.

flavor profile: thyme

This congenial herb pairs well with many other herbs—especially rosemary, parsley, sage, savory, and oregano. Because the leaves are so small, they don't require chopping. Add thyme during cooking; its powerful taste develops best at high temperatures.

sidekick: **CARROT-CUCUMBER SLAW** Combine 3 Tbsp. fresh lime juice, 2 tsp. olive oil, ¼ cup each chopped fresh mint and cilantro, and ½ tsp. salt. Cut 3 large carrots and 1 English cucumber into strips, using a julienne vegetable peeler or a mandoline. Toss with lime mixture; serve immediately.

kid favorite

Mini Taco Cups

MAKES 24 CUPS
HANDS-ON TIME: 20 MIN. **TOTAL TIME: 40 MIN.**

½ (14.1-oz.) package refrigerated piecrusts

½ (1-lb.) package mild ground pork sausage

½ lb. ground chuck

1 (8-oz.) jar taco sauce

½ cup (2 oz.) shredded Monterey Jack cheese

1 (4.5-oz.) can chopped green chiles, drained

Toppings: salsa, chopped lettuce

1. Preheat oven to 425°. Unroll piecrust on a lightly floured surface; roll into a 12-inch circle. Cut into 24 rounds using a 2-inch scalloped-edge round cutter. Press rounds into bottoms of ungreased miniature muffin cups (dough will come slightly up sides, forming a cup). Prick bottom of dough once with a fork.

2. Bake at 425° for 4 to 5 minutes or until set. Cool in pans on wire racks 15 minutes. Reduce oven temperature to 350°.

3. Meanwhile, crumble sausage and ground chuck into a microwave-safe bowl. Microwave at HIGH 1 minute, and stir. Microwave at HIGH 4 to 4½ minutes or until meat is done and no longer pink, stirring at 1-minute intervals. Drain well on paper towels. Stir together sausage mixture, taco sauce, and next 2 ingredients.

4. Fill baked piecrust cups with sausage mixture. Bake at 350° for 15 minutes or until thoroughly heated and cheese melts. Serve with desired toppings.

sidekick: **ZIPPY BLACK BEANS** Process 2 (15-oz.) cans black beans, drained and rinsed, and 1 cup vegetable broth in a food processor 10 to 15 seconds or until smooth. Sauté 1 small onion, chopped, and 1 jalapeño pepper, seeded and minced, in 1 Tbsp. hot olive oil in a large skillet 4 to 5 minutes or until tender. Add 1 garlic clove, minced, and sauté 1 minute. Add black bean purée and ½ tsp. salt, stirring until blended. Cook, stirring often, 3 minutes or until bean mixture is thoroughly heated. Stir in 1 cup (4 oz.) shredded Mexican four-cheese blend until melted.

time-saving tip:
Skip the piecrust, and serve the meat mixture in regular-size taco shells.

Sausage-and-Cheese Frittata

MAKES 6 SERVINGS
HANDS-ON TIME: 25 MIN.   TOTAL TIME: 48 MIN.

1	(12-oz.) package reduced-fat ground pork sausage	¼	tsp. salt
8	large eggs	1	Tbsp. butter
⅓	cup milk	1	cup (4 oz.) shredded 2% reduced-fat Cheddar cheese
½	tsp. pepper		

1. Preheat oven to 350°. Brown sausage in a 10-inch ovenproof non-stick skillet over medium-high heat, stirring often, 10 minutes or until meat crumbles and is no longer pink; drain and transfer to a bowl. Wipe skillet clean.

2. Whisk together eggs and next 3 ingredients until well blended.

3. Melt butter in skillet over medium heat; remove from heat, and pour half of egg mixture into skillet. Sprinkle with cooked sausage and cheese. Top with remaining egg mixture.

4. Bake at 350° for 23 to 25 minutes or until set.

sidekick: **FRUIT SALAD** Toss together fresh fruit such as raspberries, grapes, blueberries, cantaloupe, strawberries, and melon.

savvy secret
from Vanessa:

Everyone loves breakfast for dinner so keep eggs on hand for quick weeknight meals. Be sure to buy the freshest eggs available and always from a refrigerated case. At home, refrigerate immediately in the original carton, which prevents moisture loss and absorption of odor from other foods in the refrigrator. Discard any eggs with cracks.

healthy

Chile-Buttermilk Baked Chicken

MAKES 4 SERVINGS
HANDS-ON TIME: 15 MIN.   TOTAL TIME: 47 MIN.

¼ cup butter, cut into ½-inch pieces	1 (10 ¾-oz.) can reduced-fat cream of mushroom soup
4 skinned and boned chicken breasts	1 (4.5-oz.) can chopped green chiles
½ tsp. salt	1 cup (4 oz.) shredded Monterey Jack cheese
½ tsp. ground cumin	Hot cooked rice
1½ cups buttermilk, divided	¼ cup chopped fresh cilantro
½ cup all-purpose flour	

1. Preheat oven to 425°. Melt butter in a lightly greased 11- x 7-inch baking dish in oven 2 to 3 minutes.

2. Sprinkle chicken with salt and cumin. Dip chicken in ½ cup buttermilk, and dredge in flour. Arrange chicken in baking dish.

3. Bake at 425° for 15 minutes. Stir together cream of mushroom soup, chiles, and remaining 1 cup buttermilk. Pour over chicken, and bake 10 to 15 minutes or until chicken is done. Sprinkle with cheese, and bake 5 minutes or until cheese is melted. Serve chicken and sauce over hot cooked rice. Sprinkle with cilantro.

sidekick: **NUTTY GREEN BEANS** Cook 1 (12-oz.) package frozen steam-in-bag whole green beans according to package directions. Toss with 1 Tbsp. each butter, lemon zest, and lemon juice. Sprinkle with 3 Tbsp. roasted pecan-and-almond pieces; add salt and pepper to taste.

savvy secret from Vanessa:

This baked chicken recipe gives you tender, golden chicken that you dip in buttermilk and dredge in flour before baking. Then you make a sauce by adding a buttermilk-cream of mushroom soup mixture during the last 10 minutes of baking. The green chiles add extra flavor, but omit it for kids who don't like the extra kick.

time-saving tip:

Chop minutes off meal preparation by using ready-to-serve rice. The fluffy grains come fully cooked and are reheated in the microwave.

sidekick: **GOAT CHEESE CROSTINI** Stir together 2 oz. softened goat cheese, ½ tsp. chopped fresh oregano, ½ tsp. chopped fresh thyme, and ¼ tsp. freshly ground pepper in a small bowl. Spread goat cheese mixture on 8 toasted ½-inch-thick diagonally cut French bread baguette slices.

for company

Chicken and Rice

MAKES 4 SERVINGS
HANDS-ON TIME: 10 MIN.   **TOTAL TIME: 32 MIN.**

2 (8.8-oz.) pouches ready-to-serve long-grain rice	½ cup frozen green peas, thawed*
4 bacon slices, diced	1 (4-oz.) can sliced mushrooms, drained
½ cup chopped onion	¾ tsp. salt
1½ lb. skinned and boned chicken breasts, cut into ¼-inch-thick slices	¼ tsp. pepper
	Garnish: fresh parsley sprigs

1. Prepare rice according to package directions.

2. Sauté bacon in a large skillet over medium-high heat 8 minutes or until crisp; remove bacon with a slotted spoon, reserving 1 Tbsp. drippings in skillet.

3. Sauté onion in reserved hot drippings in skillet 3 minutes or until tender. Stir in chicken, and sauté 8 minutes or until chicken is done. Stir in rice, bacon, peas, and next 3 ingredients; cook, stirring occasionally, 3 minutes or until thoroughly heated. Garnish, if desired.

* 4 oz. (about 1 heaping cup) snow peas may be substituted for green peas. Microwave snow peas and ¼ cup water in a microwave-safe bowl at HIGH 2 minutes before adding to chicken mixture. Proceed with recipe as directed.

Note: We tested with Uncle Ben's Original Long Grain Ready Rice.

sidekick: **MANDARIN ORANGE SALAD** Toss I (5-oz.) head Bibb lettuce with ½ cup drained mandarin oranges. Serve with bottled ginger dressing.

table talk: Keep up with current events by declaring tonight news night. Have each person pick a favorite article from a recent newspaper, magazine, or online source and bring it to the dinner table. Have each person share his or her selection with the group and allow everyone to comment on the particular topic.

healthy

Rosemary Chicken Kabobs

MAKES 4 SERVINGS
HANDS-ON TIME: I5 MIN.   **TOTAL TIME: 40 MIN.**

⅓	cup red wine vinegar
4	garlic cloves, pressed
I	Tbsp. fresh rosemary leaves
I	tsp. salt
I	tsp. Dijon mustard
⅓	cup olive oil
I	lb. skinned and boned chicken breasts, cut into 2-inch pieces
I	large green bell pepper, cut into 2-inch pieces
I	pt. cherry tomatoes
I	(8-oz.) package fresh mushrooms
16	(6-inch) metal skewers

1. Preheat grill to 350° to 400° (medium-high) heat. Whisk together first 5 ingredients in a small bowl. Add oil in a slow, steady stream, whisking constantly, until smooth. Pour half of olive oil mixture into a shallow bowl or zip-top plastic freezer bag; add chicken, turning to coat. Cover or seal, and let stand 10 minutes. Pour remaining olive oil mixture into another bowl or freezer bag; add bell pepper, tomatoes, and mushrooms, and toss to coat. Cover or seal, and let stand 10 minutes.

2. Remove chicken and vegetables from marinade, discarding marinade. Thread chicken onto 8 skewers. Thread vegetables alternately onto remaining 8 skewers.

3. Grill kabobs, covered with grill lid, 10 to 12 minutes or until chicken is done and vegetables are tender, turning occasionally. Remove kabobs from grill. Let stand 5 minutes before serving.

flavor profile: **rosemary**

One of the most aromatic and pungent of all herbs, rosemary boasts a pronounced lemon-pine flavor. Use a light hand because its flavor is strong.

healthy

Snappy Smothered Chicken

MAKES 4 SERVINGS
HANDS-ON TIME: 30 MIN.   TOTAL TIME: 40 MIN.

1	(8-oz.) package wide egg noodles
1	tsp. paprika
1	tsp. dried thyme leaves, crumbled
½	tsp. salt
¼	tsp. pepper
3	Tbsp. butter
1	large onion, chopped
1	(16-oz.) package fresh mushrooms, sliced
2	tsp. jarred minced garlic
1	(10 ¾-oz.) can cream of mushroom soup
1	cup milk
⅓	cup dry white wine (optional)
1	whole deli-roasted chicken, cut into serving pieces
2	Tbsp. chopped fresh parsley

1. Prepare noodles according to package directions. Keep warm.

2. Stir together paprika and next 3 ingredients in a small bowl.

3. Melt butter in a large skillet over medium-high heat; add onion and mushrooms, and sauté 8 to 10 minutes or until onion is tender. Stir in garlic and paprika mixture; sauté 2 minutes. Add soup, milk, and, if desired, wine, and bring to a boil, stirring frequently. Add chicken pieces; spoon soup mixture over chicken. Reduce heat to low, and cook, covered, 10 to 15 minutes or until chicken is thoroughly heated. Stir in 1 Tbsp. parsley. Serve over hot cooked noodles. Sprinkle with remaining parsley.

sidekick: **ASIAN BROCCOLI**
Microwave 1 (12-oz.) package refrigerated broccoli florets according to package directions. Drain. Toss with ¼ cup Asian dressing. Note: We tested with Newman's Own Organic Low Fat Asian Dressing.

time-saving tip:
We added a little white wine to this recipe to dress it up a bit. If you don't have any on hand, increase the milk to 1⅓ cups.

healthy

Chipotle-Orange Chicken Legs

MAKES 4 TO 6 SERVINGS
HANDS-ON TIME: 20 MIN.   TOTAL TIME: 50 MIN.

2	Tbsp. olive oil	5	Tbsp. soy sauce, divided
6	garlic cloves, pressed		
1	Tbsp. orange zest	3	Tbsp. brown sugar
1½	tsp. kosher salt	2	lb. chicken drumsticks (about 8 drumsticks)
1	tsp. ground chipotle chile pepper	2	tsp. brown sugar
1	cup fresh orange juice, divided	2	tsp. cornstarch

1. Preheat grill to 350° to 400° (medium-high) heat. Combine first 5 ingredients, ¼ cup orange juice, 3 Tbsp. soy sauce, and 3 Tbsp. brown sugar in a shallow dish or large zip-top plastic freezer bag; add chicken. Cover or seal, and chill 10 minutes. Remove chicken from marinade, discarding marinade.

2. Grill chicken, covered with grill lid, 10 to 12 minutes on each side or until a meat thermometer inserted into thickest portion registers 165°. Remove from grill; cover with aluminum foil, and let stand 10 minutes.

3. Meanwhile, whisk together 2 tsp. brown sugar, remaining ¾ cup orange juice, and remaining 2 Tbsp. soy sauce in a small saucepan. Whisk together cornstarch and 2 tsp. water, and whisk into orange juice mixture. Bring mixture to a boil over medium heat, and cook, whisking constantly, 1 minute or until thickened. Brush sauce over chicken.

time-saving tip:

The oranges should be at room temperature before squeezing the juice to make it easier and get more juice out of them.

sidekick: **CREAMY COLESLAW** Combine 1 (16-oz.) package shredded coleslaw mix, 1 (8-oz.) container sour cream, 2 Tbsp. fresh lemon juice, and 1 tsp. salt. Cover and chill until ready to serve.

table talk: Get the dinner conversation flowing by playing a round of "worst and best." Each person at the table can share the best thing that happened to him or her that particular day, as well as the worst thing that happened that day. It's a great way for parents and children to gain insight into each other's day.

sidekick: **EASY CAESAR SALAD** Toss together romaine lettuce, freshly cracked pepper, and grated Parmesan cheese; toss with your favorite bottled Caesar dressing.

for company

Chicken Parmesan Pizza

MAKES 4 SERVINGS
HANDS-ON TIME: 15 MIN.   **TOTAL TIME: 30 MIN.**

1 (10-oz.) package frozen garlic bread loaf	1 cup (4 oz.) shredded Italian six-cheese blend
½ cup canned pizza sauce	2 Tbsp. chopped fresh basil leaves
6 deli fried chicken breast strips	

1. Preheat oven to 400°. Arrange garlic bread, buttered sides up, on a baking sheet.

2. Bake at 400° for 8 to 9 minutes or until bread is lightly browned. Spread sauce over garlic bread.

3. Cut chicken strips into ½-inch pieces, and arrange over pizza sauce. Sprinkle with cheese and basil.

4. Bake at 400° for 8 to 10 minutes or until cheese melts. Serve immediately.

cooking
for two

*These small-batch dinners are
downsized for single and double
servings without leftovers*

Pasta with Zesty Pecan Sauce

MAKES 2 SERVINGS
HANDS-ON TIME: 20 MIN. **TOTAL TIME: 35 MIN.**

- ¼ cup chopped pecans
- 2 Tbsp. chopped fresh parsley
- ½ tsp. lemon zest
- 6 oz. uncooked linguine
- ¾ cup canned quartered artichoke hearts, drained
- ¼ cup freshly grated Parmesan cheese
- 1 (3-oz.) package cream cheese, softened
- 1 Tbsp. olive oil
- 1 small garlic clove
- ¼ tsp. freshly ground pepper

1. Heat pecans in a medium-size nonstick skillet over medium-low heat, stirring often, 4 to 7 minutes or until lightly toasted and fragrant. Remove from skillet. Let cool 5 minutes. Stir together pecans, parsley, and zest.

2. Cook pasta according to package directions; drain pasta, reserving 2 Tbsp. hot pasta water.

3. Process artichoke hearts and next 5 ingredients in a food processor or blender until smooth, stopping to scrape down sides as needed. Add 2 Tbsp. reserved pasta water. Pulse 3 to 4 times or until smooth. Toss with hot cooked pasta; season with salt to taste. Top each serving with pecan mixture.

sidekick: **ITALIAN-SEASONED BREAD** Preheat oven to 350°. Split 1 (12-oz.) French bread loaf lengthwise, and brush cut sides with ½ cup melted butter. Top with 6 garlic cloves, pressed; 1 tsp. dried oregano; and ½ tsp. dried parsley flakes. Bake until lightly browned and crisp. Serve with a tossed salad or green vegetable.

know by heart

Vegetable Quesadillas

MAKES 2 SERVINGS
HANDS-ON TIME: 20 MIN.   **TOTAL TIME: 20 MIN.**

1 cup sliced yellow squash*	2 Tbsp. olive oil
½ cup sliced fresh mushrooms	½ cup (2 oz.) shredded mozzarella cheese
½ cup chopped onion	
¼ cup chopped green bell pepper	½ cup (2 oz.) shredded Cheddar cheese
½ tsp. salt	2 (8-inch) soft taco-size flour tortillas
¼ tsp. pepper	
½ tsp. hot sauce	Jarred salsa

1. Sauté first 7 ingredients in hot oil in a large skillet over medium-high heat 3 to 4 minutes or until tender. Remove vegetables to paper towels to drain, reserving oil in skillet.

2. Place 2 Tbsp. mozzarella cheese and 2 Tbsp. Cheddar cheese on half of each tortilla; top with vegetable mixture and remaining cheese. Fold tortillas over filling.

3. Cook quesadillas in reserved hot oil in skillet over medium heat 3 to 5 minutes on each side or until light golden. Serve immediately with salsa.

* 1 cup frozen sliced yellow squash, thawed, may be substituted.

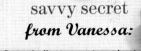

savvy secret
from Vanessa:

Store bell peppers in a plastic bag in the fridge for up to a week.

for company

Grilled Steak and Potatoes

MAKES 2 SERVINGS
HANDS-ON TIME: 30 MIN.   TOTAL TIME: 45 MIN.

4	small red potatoes (about ¾ lb.)	½	tsp. salt
1½	Tbsp. olive oil	½	tsp. freshly ground pepper
2	garlic cloves, pressed	1	(12-oz.) flank steak

1. Bring potatoes and water to cover to a boil in a medium saucepan. Cook 10 to 15 minutes or just until tender. Drain, cool 5 minutes, and cut into ½-inch-thick slices.

2. Preheat grill to 350° to 400° (medium-high) heat. Stir together olive oil and garlic. Brush half of olive oil mixture over both sides of potato slices. Sprinkle potatoes with ¼ tsp. salt and pepper. Brush both sides of steak with remaining half of olive oil mixture; sprinkle with remaining ¼ tsp. salt and pepper.

3. Grill steak, covered with grill lid, 6 to 7 minutes on each side or to desired degree of doneness. Cover loosely with aluminum foil, and let stand 10 minutes.

4. Meanwhile, grill potato slices, covered with grill lid, 3 to 4 minutes on each side or until browned.

5. Cut steak diagonally across the grain into thin strips. Serve with potatoes.

sidekick: **RED ONION RELISH** Preheat grill to 350° to 400° (medium-high) heat. Cut 1 small red onion into ¾- to 1-inch-thick slices. Brush 1½ tsp. olive oil over both sides of onion slices. Grill onion, covered with grill lid, 3 to 4 minutes on each side or until grill marks appear and onion is tender. Transfer to cutting board, and let cool slightly (about 5 minutes). Coarsely chop onion slices. Toss together onion, ⅓ cup crumbled feta cheese, ¼ cup chopped pitted oil-cured olives (about 10 olives), 2 tsp. drained capers, 2 tsp. balsamic vinegar, and ¼ tsp. freshly ground pepper.

savvy secret *from Vanessa:*

To get dinner on the table fast, make the relish first; then put the steak on. Grill the potatoes directly on the grate while the steak stands for 10 minutes. Letting the meat stand helps lock in the juices, resulting in moist, flavorful slices. Serve the Red Onion Relish warm or at room temperature. You can also top a green salad with any leftover relish and sliced steak; drizzle with a simple oil-and-vinegar salad dressing.

know by heart
Steak Parmesan

MAKES 2 SERVINGS
HANDS-ON TIME: 15 MIN.   TOTAL TIME: 35 MIN.

¼	cup fine, dry breadcrumbs	⅛	tsp. pepper
4	Tbsp. grated Parmesan cheese, divided	2	(4-oz.) cubed steaks
1	large egg, lightly beaten	2	Tbsp. vegetable oil
		½	cup pizza sauce

1. Preheat oven to 325°. Combine breadcrumbs and 2 Tbsp. cheese in a shallow bowl. Combine egg, pepper, and 1 Tbsp. water in a second shallow bowl. Dip steaks in egg mixture; dredge in breadcrumb mixture.

2. Cook steaks in hot oil in a medium skillet over medium heat 3 minutes on each side. Arrange steaks in an 8-inch square baking dish. Top with pizza sauce; bake at 325° for 20 minutes. Sprinkle with remaining 2 Tbsp. cheese.

sidekick: **GARLIC RED POTATOES** Place 2 (8-oz.) red potatoes in a medium-size microwave-safe bowl. Cover tightly with plastic wrap; fold back a small edge to allow steam to escape. Microwave at HIGH 8 minutes or until tender. Add 2 garlic cloves, minced; 2 Tbsp. butter; ¼ tsp. salt; ¼ tsp. freshly ground pepper; and 3 Tbsp. milk. Mash to desired consistency. Stir in 1 Tbsp. fresh chives.

Szechuan Beef with Broccoli

MAKES 2 SERVINGS
HANDS-ON TIME: 25 MIN.   **TOTAL TIME: 25 MIN.**

¾ lb. boneless top sirloin steak
4 tsp. canola oil, divided
2 cups fresh broccoli florets
½ tsp. dark sesame oil
1 garlic clove, minced
1 tsp. cornstarch
2½ Tbsp. Szechuan stir-fry
    and marinade

¼ cup plus 1 Tbsp. beef broth
¼ cup coarsely chopped
    dry-roasted peanuts
Hot cooked rice
Garnish: coarsely chopped
    dry-roasted peanuts

1. Cut steak diagonally across grain into very thin slices. Stir-fry steak in 2 tsp. hot canola oil in a large nonstick skillet over medium-high heat 5 minutes. Remove steak from skillet, reserving drippings in skillet.

2. Stir-fry broccoli in hot sesame oil and remaining 2 tsp. canola oil in skillet 3 minutes. Add garlic; stir-fry 30 seconds.

3. Combine cornstarch, Szechuan marinade, and beef broth, stirring until smooth. Add cornstarch mixture and steak to skillet; cook, stirring constantly, 2 minutes. Remove from heat, and stir ¼ cup peanuts. Serve over hot cooked rice. Garnish, if desired.

time-saving tip:
Buy a package of stir-fry beef tips from the grocery store.

Creamy Dijon Lamb Chops

MAKES 2 SERVINGS
HANDS-ON TIME: 30 MIN.   TOTAL TIME: 30 MIN.

4	(2-inch-thick) lamb loin chops, trimmed	1	garlic clove, minced
¼	tsp. salt	¼	cup plus 2 Tbsp. whipping cream
⅛	tsp. freshly ground pepper	1	Tbsp. Dijon mustard
1½	tsp. olive oil	⅛	tsp. dried thyme

savvy secret
from Vanessa:

There's no reason lamb shouldn't be a regular part of your menu planning with a dish as simple and delicious as this. It matches well with any sort of prepared grain: barley, couscous, quinoa, or even grits.

1. Sprinkle lamb chops with salt and pepper. Cook lamb chops in hot oil in a heavy skillet over medium heat 7 minutes on each side or until a meat thermometer inserted in thickest portion registers 150° (medium-rare). Transfer chops to a serving dish, reserving 1 Tbsp. drippings in skillet.

2. Sauté garlic in reserved drippings 30 seconds. Stir in cream, mustard, and thyme. Bring to a boil; cook, stirring constantly, 3 minutes. Spoon sauce over chops, and serve immediately.

sidekick: **GARLIC POTATO WEDGES** Preheat oven to 450°. Cut 4 small red potatoes (about ¾ lb) into 4 wedges each. Place wedges in a large bowl. Drizzle with ½ tsp. olive oil; toss well. Sprinkle with ⅛ tsp. salt, ⅛ tsp. garlic powder, and ⅛ tsp. pepper; toss to coat. Arrange wedges in a single layer on a baking sheet. Bake 20 minutes or until browned, turning once.

Skillet Sausage 'n' Rice

MAKES 2 SERVINGS
HANDS-ON TIME: 30 MIN.   **TOTAL TIME: 35 MIN.**

½   lb. smoked sausage, cut into
     ½-inch rounds
1   small green bell pepper,
     chopped (½ cup)
½   cup chopped onion
1   garlic clove, minced

½   cup chicken broth
1   (3.5-oz.) bag boil-in-bag
     brown rice
Salt and pepper to taste
Garnish: chopped fresh
     parsley

1. Sauté sausage in a large nonstick skillet over medium-high heat
8 to 10 minutes or until lightly browned. Remove sausage slices,
and drain on paper towels, reserving 1 Tbsp. drippings in skillet.

2. Add bell pepper, onion, and garlic to drippings in skillet; sauté 4
minutes or until tender. Add broth, stirring to loosen particles from
bottom of skillet; bring to a boil. Remove rice from cooking bag; add
rice, sausage, salt, and pepper to skillet. Reduce heat to medium-low;
cover and cook 5 minutes or until rice is tender. Garnish, if desired.

sidekick: **CREOLE CROSTINI** Combine 2 oz. softened cream
cheese, ½ tsp. Creole seasoning, 1 Tbsp. chopped green onion, and
¼ tsp. freshly ground pepper in a small bowl. Spread cream cheese
mixture on 4 (½-inch-thick) French bread baguette slices.

time-saving tip:
Save time by cooking a large
batch of rice on the week-
end. Store the cooked rice
in an airtight container in the
refrigerator up to 1 week;
simply reheat rice in the
microwave 60 seconds or
until thoroughly heated.

time-saving tip:

Cooked rice comes in a convenient microwavable pouch, and it's ready in just 90 seconds! You can find it in 8.8-oz. packages on the rice aisle in the supermarket.

sidekick: **ORANGE-GINGER SUGAR SNAP PEAS** Sauté 2 green onions, sliced, and ½ tsp. grated fresh ginger in 1 tsp. hot sesame oil in a large non-stick skillet over medium heat 2 minutes. Add 1 (8-oz.) package fresh sugar snap peas, and sauté 2 minutes or just until crisp-tender. Remove from heat; stir in 1 tsp. orange zest and ¼ tsp. salt.

Thai Chicken 'n' Rice Wraps

MAKES 2 SERVINGS
HANDS-ON TIME: 15 MIN.   TOTAL TIME: 15 MIN.

2	tsp. rice vinegar	1	garlic clove, pressed
1	Tbsp. plus 1 tsp. Asian chili-garlic sauce	½	cup fresh cilantro leaves, chopped
1½	tsp. grated fresh ginger	4	Bibb lettuce leaves
1	Tbsp. dark sesame oil, divided	1	cup hot cooked rice
1	cup shredded cooked chicken		

1. Combine first 3 ingredients and 1½ tsp. sesame oil in a small bowl.

2. Heat remaining 1½ tsp. oil in a medium skillet over medium heat. Add chicken and garlic; cook 2 minutes or until thoroughly heated. Stir in cilantro.

3. Place 2 lettuce leaves on each serving plate. Spoon rice onto lettuce leaves; top with chicken mixture, and roll up. Serve wraps with vinegar mixture.

kid favorite

Jamaican Chicken Burgers

MAKES 2 SERVINGS
HANDS-ON TIME: 24 MIN.   TOTAL TIME: 54 MIN.

½   lb. ground chicken*
2   Tbsp. mayonnaise
1½   tsp. grated onion
¾   tsp. Jamaican jerk seasoning
¼   tsp. salt

1½   tsp. vegetable oil
2   hamburger buns
Toppings: fresh mango slices,
      lettuce leaves, sweet-hot
      pickles, tomato slices

1. Combine first 5 ingredients in a large bowl. Shape into 2 (3-inch) patties. Cover and chill 30 minutes.

2. Cook patties in hot oil in a large nonstick skillet over medium-high heat 7 to 8 minutes on each side or until done. Serve on buns with desired toppings.

* Ground pork may be substituted.

sidekick: **JERK-SPICED SWEET POTATO FRIES** Coat frozen sweet potato fries with olive oil and Jamaican jerk seasoning; bake according to package directions.

flavor profile: Jamaican jerk seasoning

Jerk seasoning is pungent—the longer the meat marinates, the more flavorful and spicy it becomes. This spice rub pairs well with poultry.

sidekick: ANGEL HAIR
PASTA Cook 4 oz. angel hair pasta according to package directions. Meanwhile, pulse 1 (8-oz.) whole wheat bread slice in a food processor 5 times or until coarse crumbles measure ½ cup. Combine cooked pasta, breadcrumbs, 1 Tbsp. butter, 2 tsp. chopped fresh parsley, ¼ tsp. salt, and ⅛ tsp. pepper; toss gently. Serve immediately.

kid favorite

Chicken Parmesan

MAKES 2 SERVINGS
HANDS-ON TIME: 20 MIN.   **TOTAL TIME: 36 MIN.**

1 cup Italian-seasoned breadcrumbs	1 Tbsp. olive oil
2 Tbsp. all-purpose flour	1½ cups pasta sauce
½ tsp. ground red pepper	1 cup (4 oz.) shredded mozzarella cheese
2 skinned and boned chicken breasts	¼ cup grated Parmesan cheese
2 egg whites, lightly beaten	Garnish: basil leaves

1. Preheat oven to 400°. Combine first 3 ingredients in a small bowl.

2. Place chicken between 2 sheets of heavy-duty plastic wrap, and flatten to ¼-inch thickness, using a rolling pin or the flat side of a meat mallet. Dip chicken in egg whites; dredge in breadcrumb mixture. Dip again in egg whites, and dredge again in breadcrumb mixture.

3. Cook chicken in hot oil in a large skillet over medium heat 3 minutes on each side or until done.

4. Place chicken breasts in a single layer in a lightly greased 8-inch square baking dish. Top with pasta sauce and cheeses. Bake at 400° for 10 minutes or until cheese is melted. Garnish, if desired.

Glazed Roasted Chicken Thighs

MAKES 2 SERVINGS
HANDS-ON TIME: 10 MIN.   **TOTAL TIME: 8 HR., 40 MIN.**

¼	cup teriyaki sauce	½	tsp. salt
2	Tbsp. frozen orange juice concentrate, thawed	¼	tsp. freshly ground pepper
1½	Tbsp. dark sesame oil	4	skinned, bone-in chicken thighs
2	garlic cloves, minced	½	tsp. sesame seeds

1. Stir together first 6 ingredients. Reserve half of teriyaki sauce mixture; store in an airtight container in refrigerator up to 2 days.

2. Pour remaining mixture into a large shallow dish or zip-top plastic freezer bag; add chicken. Cover or seal, and chill 8 hours, turning occasionally. Preheat oven to 450°. Remove chicken from marinade, discarding marinade. Place chicken on an aluminum foil-lined 15- x 10-inch jelly-roll pan.

3. Bake at 450° for 30 minutes or until a meat thermometer inserted in thickest portion of chicken registers 165°, basting once with reserved teriyaki sauce mixture. Skim fat from pan juices; stir remaining juices into reserved teriyaki sauce mixture. Brush chicken with mixture. Sprinkle with sesame seeds. Serve immediately.

sidekick: **JULIENNE**

CARROTS Cut 3 medium carrots into 2½ x ¼-inch strips. Blanch carrots for 1 minute; drain. Sauté carrots over medium heat in 1 Tbsp. of olive oil for 4 to 5 minutes until heated. Sprinkle with 1 Tbsp. chopped cilantro.

kid favorite

Turkey Tetrazzini

MAKES 2 SERVINGS
HANDS-ON TIME: 30 MIN.   **TOTAL TIME: 30 MIN.**

1½ cups diced deli turkey breast (about ½ pound)*

½ cup chopped onion

¼ cup milk

1 (10 ¾-oz.) can cream of mushroom soup

¾ cup (3 oz.) shredded sharp Cheddar cheese

4 oz. spaghetti, cooked

2 Tbsp. chopped fresh parsley

⅛ tsp. pepper

1 (2-oz.) jar diced pimiento, drained

1. Sauté turkey and onion in a large nonstick skillet coated with cooking spray over medium-high heat 3 minutes or until onion is tender.

2. Stir in milk, soup, and cheese; reduce heat to low, and cook, stirring constantly, 4 minutes or until cheese melts and mixture is smooth. Stir in spaghetti and remaining ingredients; cook 2 to 3 minutes or until thoroughly heated.

* Diced ham may be substituted.

healthy

Shrimp Scampi

MAKES 2 SERVINGS
HANDS-ON TIME: 10 MIN.   **TOTAL TIME: 10 MIN.**

1½ lb. peeled jumbo raw shrimp (16/20 count)*	1½ Tbsp. fresh lemon juice
1½ Tbsp. jarred minced garlic	½ tsp. salt
1½ Tbsp. olive oil	Dash of ground red pepper
¼ cup finely chopped fresh flat-leaf parsley	

1. Devein shrimp, if desired.

2. Sauté garlic in hot oil in a medium-size nonstick skillet over medium-high heat 1 minute.

3. Add shrimp to skillet, and cook, stirring occasionally, 5 minutes or just until shrimp turn pink.

4. Remove skillet from heat; stir in parsley and remaining ingredients.

* 2¼ lb. unpeeled jumbo raw shrimp may be substituted. Peel shrimp prior to cooking.

savvy secret *from Vanessa:*

Serve this dish with a toasted French bread baguette slices or ½-cup portions of warm angel hair pasta. It's a winner either way.

healthy

Spicy Grouper Fillets

MAKES 2 SERVINGS
HANDS-ON TIME: 21 MIN.   TOTAL TIME: 21 MIN.

3	Tbsp. all-purpose flour		1	garlic clove, crushed
½	tsp. ground red pepper		1	tsp. olive oil
¼	tsp. salt			Lemon wedges (optional)
2	(6-oz.) grouper fillets			
	(about 1 inch thick)			

1. Combine first 3 ingredients in a large zip-top plastic freezer bag. Add fish; turn gently to coat.

2. Sauté garlic in hot oil in a large nonstick skillet over medium heat 30 seconds; discard garlic, reserving oil in skillet. Add fish to hot oil; cook 8 to 9 minutes on each side or until fish flakes with a fork. Serve with lemon wedges, if desired.

sidekick: **SAUTÉED ZUCCHINI AND BELL PEPPER** Sauté 1 medium zucchini, cut into 2-inch pieces; 1 cup refrigerated prechopped green, red, and yellow bell pepper; 1 minced garlic clove; and ¼ tsp. salt in 1 tsp. hot oil in a large nonstick skillet over medium-high heat 7 minutes.

savvy secret
from Vanessa:

Select grouper fillets that are as uniform in thickness as possible. If a fillet is uneven, loosely fold under the thin end to even out the thickness. If you can't find grouper, substitute a firm white fish, such as cod, snapper, or tilapia.

204   *What's for Supper*

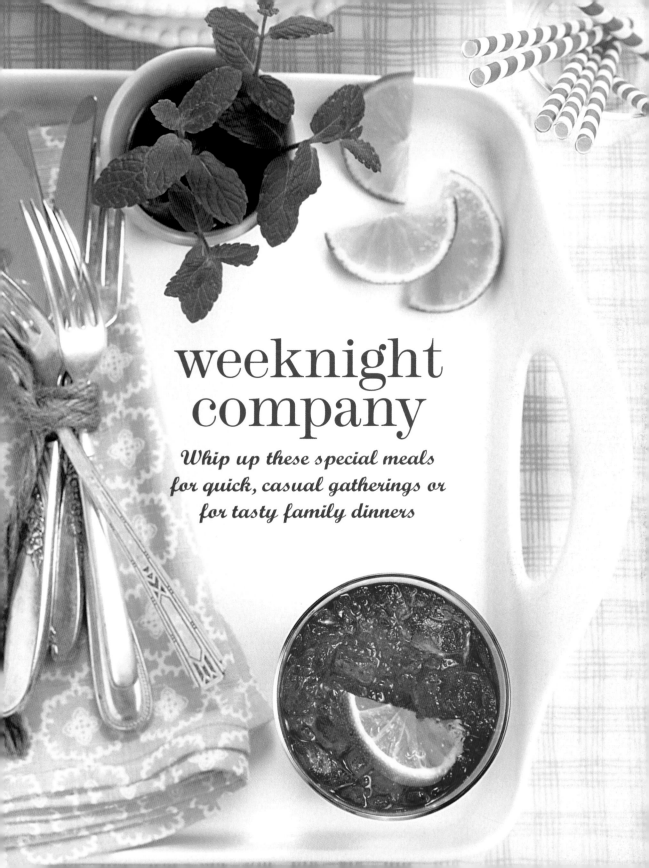

weeknight company

*Whip up these special meals
for quick, casual gatherings or
for tasty family dinners*

know by heart

Tomato-and-Corn Pizza

MAKES 4 SERVINGS
HANDS-ON TIME: 10 MIN.   TOTAL TIME: 44 MIN.

2 small plum tomatoes, sliced	½ cup fresh corn kernels
¼ tsp. salt	¼ cup grated Parmesan
⅛ tsp. freshly ground pepper	cheese
1 (14-oz.) package prebaked	1 tsp. sugar
Italian pizza crust	8 oz. fresh mozzarella cheese,
Parchment paper	sliced
⅓ cup reduced-fat refrigerated	3 Tbsp. fresh whole or torn
pesto sauce	basil leaves

1. Preheat oven to 450°. Place tomato slices on paper towels. Sprinkle with salt and pepper; let stand 20 minutes.

2. Place pizza crust on a parchment paper-lined baking sheet; spread with pesto. Stir together corn, Parmesan, and sugar. Top pizza with corn mixture, tomatoes, and mozzarella slices.

3. Bake at 450° for 14 minutes or until cheese is melted and golden. Remove from oven, and top with basil leaves.

Note: We tested with Boboli Original Pizza Crust.

savvy secret
from Vanessa:

Planning on having friends over? Impress them with this hearty pizza. The recipe serves four, so double it to serve eight. Most ovens can handle two (12-inch) pizzas at a time.

for company

Herbed Tomato Tart

MAKES 6 SERVINGS
HANDS-ON TIME: 25 MIN.   TOTAL TIME: I HR., I0 MIN.

2	medium tomatoes, thinly sliced (about ¾ lb.)	I	(4-oz.) package crumbled feta cheese
½	pt. assorted small tomatoes, halved	¼	cup finely chopped chives
¾	tsp. salt, divided	I	garlic clove, minced
I	(I7.3-oz.) package frozen puff pastry sheets, thawed	¼	cup finely chopped assorted fresh herbs
I	(8-oz.) package shredded mozzarella cheese	I	Tbsp. olive oil

1. Preheat oven to 400°. Place tomatoes in a single layer on paper towels; sprinkle with ½ tsp. salt. Let stand 30 minutes. Pat dry with paper towels.

2. Meanwhile, roll I pastry sheet into a I4-inch square on a lightly floured surface; place on an ungreased baking sheet. Cut 4 (I2- x I-inch) strips from remaining pastry sheet, and place strips along outer edges of pastry square, forming a border. Reserve remaining pastry for another use.

3. Bake at 400° for I4 minutes or until browned.

4. Sprinkle pastry with mozzarella cheese and next 3 ingredients. Top with tomatoes in a single layer. Sprinkle tomatoes with herbs and remaining ¼ tsp. salt; drizzle with oil.

5. Bake at 400° for I4 to I5 minutes or until cheese melts. Serve immediately.

savvy secret
from Vanessa:

We used basil, dill, thyme, and parsley, but just about any combination of herbs that pairs well with tomatoes—such as oregano and tarragon—would also work.

Mexicali Meatless Tostadas

MAKES 6 SERVINGS
HANDS-ON TIME: 10 MIN.   TOTAL TIME: 15 MIN.

1 (12-oz.) package frozen meatless burger crumbles	1 (16-oz.) can refried beans
3 tsp. taco seasoning	1 (8-oz.) package shredded Mexican four-cheese blend
12 tostada shells	Topping: pico de gallo
1 (8.5-oz.) pouch ready-to-serve whole-grain Santa Fe rice	

1. Preheat oven to 425°. Prepare crumbles according to package directions. Stir taco seasoning into hot crumble mixture. Prepare tostada shells and rice according to package directions.

2. Layer refried beans, crumble mixture, and rice on tostada shells. Sprinkle with cheese. Bake at 425° for 5 to 6 minutes or until cheese is melted. Serve with topping.

Note: We tested with MorningStar Farms Meal Starters Grillers Recipe Crumbles.

sidekick: **AVOCADO MASH** Coarsely mash 2 ripe avocados. Toss with ¼ cup chopped red onion, 1 minced garlic clove, 3 Tbsp. fresh cilantro leaves, 2 Tbsp. fresh lime juice, and ½ tsp. salt.

savvy secret
from Vanessa:

Try some of my favorite meat-free specialties. Whip up a high-protein omelet filled with sautéed fresh spinach, tomatoes, and feta cheese. Or try a grilled portobello mushroom "burger" with your favorite toppings and a hearty bun. Another favorite meal idea is to top a baked potato with steamed broccoli, cauliflower, and shredded pepper Jack cheese.

know by heart

Fresh Tomato-and-Asparagus Gnocchi

MAKES 4 SERVINGS
HANDS-ON TIME: 25 MIN.   TOTAL TIME: 30 MIN.

1	lb. fresh asparagus	½	cup chopped fresh basil
1	(16-oz.) package gnocchi	1	tsp. salt
½	cup chopped sweet onion	½	tsp. freshly ground pepper
2	Tbsp. olive oil		Grated Parmesan cheese
4	garlic cloves, pressed		
4	large tomatoes, seeded and chopped		

1. Snap off and discard tough ends of asparagus. Cut asparagus into 2-inch pieces. Fill a 3-qt. saucepan three-fourths full with salted water. Bring to a boil; add asparagus and gnocchi, and cook 2 to 4 minutes or until tender. Drain.

2. Sauté onion in hot oil in a medium skillet over medium-high heat 5 to 6 minutes or until tender; add garlic, and cook 1 minute. Add tomatoes, and cook 3 to 5 minutes. Stir in basil, salt, pepper, and asparagus mixture. Sprinkle each serving with Parmesan cheese; serve immediately.

sidekick: **DOUBLE CHEESE SANDWICHES** Brush softened butter on 1 side of 8 whole grain bread slices. Place 4 bread slices, buttered sides down, on a griddle. Top each with 1 Havarti cheese slice, 1 Swiss cheese slice, and remaining bread slices, buttered sides up. Cook over medium heat 1 to 2 minutes on each side or until golden and cheese is melted.

flavor profile: heirloom tomatoes

These Southern garden favorites are remarkably flavorful and colorful
compared with their grocery store counterparts. They vary widely in color.
You'll find them in the following hues: red, orange, gold, taxi yellow, almost
white, pink, purplish black, and green.

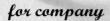

Black-eyed Pea Cakes with Heirloom Tomatoes and Slaw

MAKES 3 SERVINGS
HANDS-ON TIME: 20 MIN.   TOTAL TIME: 20 MIN.

1 (15-oz.) can seasoned black-eyed peas, undrained	1 tsp. salt, divided
2 garlic cloves, pressed	⅓ cup sour cream
1 (6-oz.) package buttermilk cornbread mix	1 tsp. lime zest
1 large egg, lightly beaten	1 Tbsp. fresh lime juice
¼ cup sour cream	2 tsp. sugar
1½ tsp. Southwest chipotle salt-free seasoning blend	1 (12-oz.) package fresh broccoli slaw
	2 large heirloom tomatoes, cut into ¼-inch-thick slices

1. Coarsely mash peas with fork. Stir in garlic, next 4 ingredients, and ½ tsp. salt. Stir until blended.

2. Spoon about ⅓ cup batter for each cake onto a hot lightly greased griddle. Cook cakes 2 minutes or until edges look dry and cooked; turn and cook 2 more minutes.

3. Stir together ⅓ cup sour cream, next 3 ingredients, and remaining ½ tsp. salt in a large bowl. Stir in slaw.

4. Place 2 cooked cakes on a serving plate; top cakes with 2 tomato slices. Add salt and pepper to taste. Top with slaw; serve immediately.

Zucchini-and-Spinach Lasagna

MAKES 4 TO 6 SERVINGS
HANDS-ON TIME: 15 MIN.   **TOTAL TIME: 55 MIN.**

1 (8-oz.) container whipped chive-and-onion cream cheese	2 Tbsp. olive oil
1 (15-oz.) container ricotta cheese	1 (10-oz.) package fresh spinach
⅓ cup chopped fresh basil	2 garlic cloves, pressed
1 tsp. salt	6 no-boil lasagna noodles
5 medium zucchini, thinly sliced (about 2½ lb.)	1 (7-oz.) package shredded mozzarella cheese
	Garnish: fresh basil leaves

time-saving tip:
Reduce meal prep time by using jarred, minced garlic cloves instead of pressing the garlic yourself. Look for it in the refrigerated produce section at your supermarket.

1. Preheat oven to 425°. Stir together first 4 ingredients in a bowl.

2. Sauté zucchini in hot oil in a large skillet over medium-high heat 3 to 4 minutes or until lightly browned. Add spinach; gently toss until wilted. Add garlic; cook 1 minute.

3. Spoon one-third of vegetables into a lightly greased 9-inch square baking dish; top with 2 noodles and one-third of ricotta mixture. Repeat twice. Sprinkle with mozzarella.

4. Bake, covered with lightly greased aluminum foil, at 425° for 25 to 30 minutes or until bubbly and noodles are tender. Uncover and bake 5 to 10 minutes or until golden. Let stand 10 minutes. Garnish, if desired.

healthy

Mexican Brisket Salad

MAKES 4 SERVINGS
HANDS-ON TIME: 15 MIN.   TOTAL TIME: 15 MIN.

4	oz. corn tortilla chips
1	head iceberg lettuce, shredded
1	lb. chopped barbecued beef brisket (without sauce), warmed
1	(15-oz.) can black beans, drained and rinsed
1	avocado, diced
¼	cup finely chopped red onion
1	jalapeño pepper, sliced
4	tsp. chopped fresh cilantro
½	cup bottled lite lime vinaigrette

Toppings: shredded pepper Jack cheese, chopped tomato, pico de gallo

1. Divide chips among 4 plates; top with one-fourth of lettuce, brisket, and next 5 ingredients. Drizzle each salad with 2 Tbsp. vinaigrette. Serve with desired toppings.

sidekick: **GUACAMOLE** Cut 2 ripe avocados in half. Scoop avocado pulp into bowl; mash just until chunky. Stir in 2 Tbsp. finely chopped red onion; 2 Tbsp. lime juice; ½ medium-size jalapeño pepper, seeded and chopped; 1 garlic clove, pressed; and ¾ tsp. salt. Serve immediately.

flavor profile: jalapeño peppers

These fresh peppers add a spicy kick. If you want the peppers to be a bit milder, remove the seeds and white membranes.

for company

Cajun Steaks with Louisiana Slaw

MAKES 4 SERVINGS
HANDS-ON TIME: 15 MIN. **TOTAL TIME: 27 MIN.**

½ cup mayonnaise

1 Tbsp. apple cider vinegar

2 Tbsp. Creole mustard, divided

1½ tsp. Cajun seasoning, divided

1 (16-oz.) package shredded coleslaw mix

4 (6-oz.) chuck-eye steaks

½ tsp. salt

1 medium-size red onion, cut into ½-inch-thick slices

savvy secret
from Vanessa:

Tightly wrapped and refrigerated, raw beef will last three to four days. At that point, it should be cooked or frozen. Cooked, it will keep in the refrigerator 3 to 4 days longer; frozen, it's best used within 2 months.

1. Stir together mayonnaise, vinegar, 1 Tbsp. Creole mustard, and 1 tsp. Cajun seasoning in a medium bowl until blended. Stir in coleslaw. Cover and chill.

2. Meanwhile, brush steaks with remaining 1 Tbsp. mustard, and sprinkle with salt and remaining ½ tsp. Cajun seasoning. Heat a grill pan over medium-high heat. Cook steaks in pan 6 minutes on each side or to desired degree of doneness. Cook onion 5 minutes on each side. Serve steak and onions immediately with coleslaw.

sidekick: **ROASTED POTATOES** Serve with roasted potato wedges from the frozen food aisle. Cook potato wedges according to package directions. Sprinkle with kosher salt.

for company

Grilled Steak-Corn-Spinach Salad

MAKES 6 SERVINGS
HANDS-ON TIME: 30 MIN.   TOTAL TIME: 30 MIN.

2	lb. rib-eye steak	1	(5-oz.) package fresh baby spinach
4	Tbsp. olive oil	2	ripe avocados, thinly sliced
4	garlic cloves, pressed	1	red grapefruit, sectioned
1¼	tsp. salt		Bottled peppercorn Ranch dressing
½	tsp. freshly ground pepper		
4	ears fresh corn, husks removed		

1. Preheat grill to 350° to 400° (medium-high) heat. Rub steak with 2 Tbsp. olive oil and next 3 ingredients. Brush corn with remaining 2 Tbsp. olive oil.

2. Grill steak and corn at the same time, covered with grill lid, 7 to 8 minutes, turning steak once and turning corn every 4 to 5 minutes. Let steak stand 10 minutes.

3. Meanwhile, hold each grilled cob upright on a cutting board, and carefully cut downward, cutting kernels from cob. Discard cobs. Thinly slice steak.

4. Layer spinach, grilled corn kernels, steak, avocados, and grapefruit on serving plates. Serve with peppercorn Ranch dressing.

savvy secret
from Vanessa:

This recipe provides the perfect opportunity to visit the farmers' market for fresh ingredients. To find markets in your area, visit localharvest.org. At day's end, vendors are packing up and more willing to cut you a deal. Stash a cooler with ice packs in your trunk. Produce will stay fresh even if you run a few errands before heading home.

Beef Lombardi

MAKES 6 SERVINGS
HANDS-ON TIME: 25 MIN.   TOTAL TIME: 50 MIN.

1 (8-oz.) package medium egg noodles	1 (3-oz.) package cream cheese, softened
1 lb. lean ground beef	½ cup sour cream
1½ tsp. salt, divided	4 green onions, chopped
½ tsp. dried Italian seasoning	½ cup (2 oz.) shredded Italian six-cheese blend
1 (6-oz.) can tomato paste	
1 (14½-oz.) can diced fire-roasted tomatoes	

1. Preheat oven to 350°. Prepare egg noodles according to package directions.

2. Meanwhile, sprinkle ground beef with 1¼ tsp. salt and ½ tsp. Italian seasoning. Cook beef in a large skillet over medium heat, stirring often, 5 to 6 minutes or until meat crumbles and is no longer pink.

3. Stir in tomato paste, and cook 2 minutes; stir in tomatoes, ½ cup water, and remaining ¼ tsp. salt. Reduce heat to low, and simmer 8 minutes.

4. Microwave cream cheese in a microwave-safe bowl at HIGH 20 seconds. Stir in sour cream and green onions. Stir cream cheese mixture into hot cooked noodles.

5. Place noodle mixture in bottom of a lightly greased 11-x 7-inch baking dish. Top with beef mixture; sprinkle with shredded Italian cheese.

6. Bake at 350° for 25 minutes or until hot and bubbly.

time-saving tip:

Freeze unbaked casserole up to 1 month, if desired. Thaw in refrigerator overnight. Bake as directed.

To lighten: Substitute low-fat or fat-free sour cream and 2% reduced-fat Cheddar cheese.

kid favorite

Pan-Fried Pork Chops with Roasted Green Beans and Pecans

MAKES 4 SERVINGS
HANDS-ON TIME: 30 MIN.   TOTAL TIME: 30 MIN.

2	(12-oz.) packages fresh cut green beans	¼	cup freshly grated Parmesan cheese
1	Tbsp. olive oil	1	Tbsp. lemon zest
1	tsp. salt, divided	1	tsp. chopped fresh thyme
4	(4- to 6-oz.) bone-in center-cut pork chops	¼	cup vegetable oil
¼	tsp. pepper	¼	cup chopped pecans
½	cup panko (Japanese breadcrumbs)	½	Tbsp. butter

1. Preheat oven to 450°. Drain and rinse beans. Combine beans, olive oil, and ¾ tsp. salt in a large bowl, tossing to coat. Spread beans in a single layer in a jelly-roll pan. Bake 18 to 20 minutes or until beans are tender and slightly browned.

2. Meanwhile, sprinkle pork chops with pepper and remaining ¼ tsp. salt.

3. Stir together breadcrumbs and next 3 ingredients in a large shallow dish. Dredge pork chops in breadcrumb mixture.

4. Cook chops in hot oil in a large skillet over medium heat 5 to 6 minutes on each side or until done.

5. Stir pecans and butter into beans; bake 5 to 6 more minutes or until pecans are golden. Serve pork chops with green beans.

table talk: Casual weeknight suppers with friends provide the perfect opportunity to learn more about your guests. Take turns going around the table to discuss the favorite place that each person has visited or the best meal ever eaten. You might just discover a place you need to add to *your* travel wish list.

kid favorite

Oven-Fried Pork Chops

MAKES 4 SERVINGS
HANDS-ON TIME: 10 MIN.   TOTAL TIME: 21 MIN.

4	(½-inch-thick) pork chops (about 1½ lb.)
1	tsp. salt
½	tsp. black pepper
⅛	tsp. ground red pepper

1 sleeve saltine crackers, crushed (about 1 cup crushed)

1 large egg, lightly beaten

Vegetable cooking spray

1. Preheat oven to 425°. Sprinkle pork chops with salt and next 2 ingredients. Place cracker crumbs in a shallow dish.

2. Dip chops in egg, and dredge in cracker crumbs. Place on a lightly greased rack on a baking sheet. Spray chops with cooking spray.

3. Bake at 425° for 8 to 10 minutes or until a meat thermometer inserted in thickest portion registers 145°. Let chops stand 3 minutes before serving.

sidekick: **SPINACH SALAD WITH BALSAMIC DRESSING** Whisk together 2 Tbsp. minced shallots, 1 Tbsp. olive oil, 1 Tbsp. balsamic vinegar, and ⅛ tsp. salt in a large bowl. Add 6 cups loosely packed fresh baby spinach; toss well.

time-saving tip: To quickly make cracker crumbs, place the saltine crackers in a zip-top plastic freezer bag. Seal tightly. Roll over the bag with a rolling pin several times to crush the crackers. Make batches of your own coating ahead of time.

healthy

Grilled Pork Tenderloin with Squash Medley

MAKES 4 SERVINGS
HANDS-ON TIME: 10 MIN.   TOTAL TIME: 50 MIN.

1 (1-lb.) pork tenderloin	1 Tbsp. honey
2 tsp. salt, divided	1 garlic clove, minced
¾ tsp. pepper, divided	2 yellow squash
2 Tbsp. Dijon mustard	2 zucchini
1 Tbsp. chopped fresh thyme	1 tsp. olive oil
1 Tbsp. olive oil	1 tsp. fresh thyme leaves

1. Preheat grill to 350° to 400° (medium-high) heat. Remove silver skin from tenderloin, leaving a thin layer of fat.

2. Sprinkle pork with 1 tsp. salt and ½ tsp. pepper. Combine mustard and next 4 ingredients. Rub mustard mixture on pork; cover and let stand 10 minutes.

3. Preheat oven to 450°. Cut squash and zucchini into ½-inch slices; cut into half moons. Toss with 1 tsp. olive oil and remaining 1 tsp. salt and ¼ tsp. pepper. Place on an aluminum foil-lined jelly-roll pan, and bake for 20 minutes or until tender.

4. Meanwhile, grill pork, covered with grill lid, 10 to 12 minutes on each side or until a meat thermometer inserted into thickest portion registers 145°. Remove from grill; cover with foil, and let stand 10 minutes. Slice pork, and serve with squash medley. Sprinkle with thyme.

sidekick: **CREAMY MASHED POTATOES WITH CHIVES** Prepare 1 (24-oz.) package frozen steam-and-mash potatoes according to package directions. Stir in ⅓ cup whipped chive-flavored cream cheese. Add pepper to taste and 2 Tbsp. melted butter.

Grilled Peppers and Sausage with Cheese Grits

MAKES 6 SERVINGS
HANDS-ON TIME: 30 MIN.   TOTAL TIME: 37 MIN.

2	medium-size red bell peppers, cut into quarters	1	cup uncooked quick-cooking grits
2	medium-size sweet onions, cut into quarters	2	Tbsp. butter
2	Tbsp. olive oil	1	cup grated Parmesan cheese
1	tsp. fresh thyme leaves	⅓	cup chopped fresh basil
1	tsp. salt, divided	½	tsp. freshly ground pepper
1	(19.76-oz.) package garlic pork sausage links		
2	(14.5-oz.) cans chicken broth		

1. Preheat grill to 350° to 400° (medium-high) heat. Toss peppers and onions with olive oil, thyme, and ½ tsp. salt.

2. Grill pepper mixture and sausage at the same time, covered with grill lid. Grill pepper mixture, turning occasionally, 8 to 10 minutes or until wilted. Grill sausage 5 minutes on each side or until done.

3. Bring chicken broth, ½ cup water, and remaining ½ tsp. salt to a boil in a 3-qt. saucepan; slowly stir in grits, reduce heat, and simmer 12 minutes or until thickened and creamy, stirring often. Remove from heat, and stir in butter and next 3 ingredients.

4. Coarsely chop peppers and onions, and slice sausage into 1-inch pieces. Serve pepper-and-sausage mixture over hot cooked grits.

Note: We tested with Johnsonville Irish O'Garlic Sausage.

flavor profile: quick-cooking grits

A down-home favorite found in many dishes, quick grits are ground fine and cook in 5 minutes. Store grits in the freezer. It keeps them fresh and always handy.

for company

Onion-Topped Sausage 'n' Mashed Potato Casserole

MAKES 6 SERVINGS
HANDS-ON TIME: 20 MIN.   **TOTAL TIME: 1 HR., 5 MIN.**

1 (19.5-oz.) package sweet ground turkey sausage, casings removed*	1 (24-oz.) package refrigerated garlic-flavored mashed potatoes
2 (14.5-oz.) cans diced tomatoes in sauce	1 (8-oz.) package shredded Italian five-cheese blend
¼ cup loosely packed fresh basil leaves, chopped**	¼ tsp. dried Italian seasoning
1 shallot, chopped	1 cup French fried onions
1 tsp. salt-free garlic-and-herb seasoning	

time-saving tip:

To remove the sausage casings, simply freeze the sausage overnight, and then let it partially thaw in the refrigerator. Cut a slit down one side of the partially frozen sausages, and peel the casings right off.

1. Preheat oven to 350°. Brown sausage in a large skillet over medium-high heat, stirring often, 6 to 8 minutes or until meat crumbles and is no longer pink; drain.

2. Stir in tomatoes and next 3 ingredients, and cook, stirring occasionally, 5 minutes. Transfer sausage mixture to a lightly greased 11- x 7-inch baking dish.

3. Stir together mashed potatoes, cheese, and Italian seasoning in a large bowl. (Mixture will be dry.) Spread potato mixture over sausage mixture in baking dish.

4. Bake at 350° for 35 to 40 minutes or until bubbly. Top with fried onions, and bake 5 more minutes. Let stand 5 minutes before serving.

* 1 (1¼-lb.) package ground chicken sausage may be substituted.

** ½ tsp. dried basil may be substituted.

Note: We tested with Bob Evans Garlic Mashed Potatoes and Mrs. Dash Garlic & Herb Seasoning Blend.

One-Dish Chicken Pasta

MAKES 6 SERVINGS
HANDS-ON TIME: 30 MIN.   **TOTAL TIME: 30 MIN.**

1	(12-oz.) package farfalle (bow-tie) pasta	3	cups chopped cooked chicken
5	Tbsp. butter, divided	1	cup (4 oz.) shredded Parmesan cheese
1	medium onion, chopped	1	tsp. pepper
1	medium-size red bell pepper, chopped	½	tsp. salt
1	(8-oz.) package fresh mushrooms, quartered	Toppings: toasted sliced almonds, chopped fresh
⅓	cup all-purpose flour		flat-leaf parsley, shredded
3	cups chicken broth		Parmesan cheese
2	cups milk		

1. Prepare pasta according to package directions. Meanwhile, melt 2 Tbsp. butter in a Dutch oven over medium heat. Add onion and bell pepper; sauté 5 minutes or until tender. Add mushrooms; sauté 4 minutes. Remove from Dutch oven.

2. Melt remaining 3 Tbsp. butter in Dutch oven over low heat; whisk in flour until smooth. Cook, whisking constantly, 1 minute. Gradually whisk in chicken broth and milk; cook over medium heat, whisking constantly, 5 to 7 minutes or until thickened and bubbly.

3. Stir chicken, sautéed vegetables, and hot cooked pasta into sauce. Add cheese, pepper, and salt. Serve with desired toppings.

flavor profile: bell pepper

Bell peppers are at their best from July through September. Look for firm, nicely colored fruit that is fragrant at the stem end. Avoid peppers that are damp, because they can mold. Store peppers in a plastic bag in the refrigerator up to a week. They can also be sliced or chopped and frozen in freezer bags up to 6 months.

savvy secret from Vanessa:

Toasting intensifies the flavor of nuts. But the nut is a mighty delicate thing—in an oven it can go from perfectly toasty to charred in seconds. This has happened to every one of our Test Kitchen cooks. For perfect results, arrange nuts in a single layer on a heavy baking sheet, and bake at 350° for 2 to 5 minutes, stirring halfway through bake time, frequently so the nuts toast evenly—they tend to brown on the bottom more quickly. They're done when they've turned golden brown and smell fragrant and toasty.

savvy secret
from Vanessa:

A clean grill invites spur-of-the-moment cooking. It's a lot easier to clean it immediately after use. Remove racks from the grill, and scrape off stuck-on particles using a stiff grill brush or scouring pads. Clean racks with soapy water; rinse and dry thoroughly. Coat racks with vegetable cooking spray. Clean out the firebox. Replace racks, and cover with grill lid.

for company

Pepper and Chicken Nachos

MAKES 4 SERVINGS
HANDS-ON TIME: 18 MIN.   **TOTAL TIME: 37 MIN.**

4	garlic cloves, pressed	2	cups chopped deli-roasted
¼	cup cider vinegar		chicken
⅓	cup olive oil	1	(15½-oz.) can black-eyed
½	tsp. ground cumin		peas, drained and rinsed
½	tsp. salt	1	(7.5-oz.) package sliced
½	tsp. freshly ground pepper		sharp Cheddar cheese
4	medium-size bell peppers,	⅓	cup loosely packed fresh
	cut into 2-inch pieces		cilantro leaves, chopped

1. Preheat grill to 350° to 400° (medium-high) heat. Combine garlic and next 5 ingredients. Reserve 3 Tbsp. garlic mixture. Pour remaining garlic mixture into a large shallow dish; add peppers, turning to coat. Cover and chill 15 minutes, turning once. Remove peppers from marinade, reserving marinade for basting.

2. Grill peppers, covered with grill lid, 8 to 10 minutes or until peppers blister and are tender, turning occasionally and basting with marinade.

3. Preheat broiler with oven rack 4 inches from heat. Combine chicken and peas with reserved 3 Tbsp. garlic mixture. Place peppers in a single layer on a lightly greased rack in an aluminum foil-lined broiler pan. Quarter cheese slices. Top each pepper with chicken mixture and one cheese quarter.

4. Broil 4 to 5 minutes or until cheese is melted. Remove from oven, sprinkle with cilantro, and serve immediately.

kid favorite

Grilled Chicken with Corn and Slaw

MAKES 4 SERVINGS
HANDS-ON TIME: 30 MIN.   **TOTAL TIME: 30 MIN.**

1	cup mayonnaise	4	ears fresh corn, husks
¼	cup chopped fresh cilantro		removed
6	Tbsp. white wine vinegar,	¼	cup melted butter
	divided	1	(10-oz.) package shredded
¾	tsp. salt, divided		coleslaw mix
⅛	tsp. pepper	3	Tbsp. olive oil
4	skinned and boned chicken	½	tsp. sugar
	breasts (about 1 lb.)	¼	tsp. pepper

1. Combine mayonnaise, cilantro, 3 Tbsp. vinegar, ¼ tsp. salt, and ⅛ tsp. pepper in a small bowl. Reserve ¾ cup mayonnaise mixture. Brush chicken with remaining ¼ cup mayonnaise mixture.

2. Preheat grill to 350° to 400° (medium-high) heat. Grill chicken and corn at the same time, covered with grill lid. Grill chicken 7 to 10 minutes on each side or until done; grill corn 14 to 20 minutes or until done, turning every 4 to 5 minutes and basting with melted butter.

3. Toss coleslaw mix with oil, sugar, ¼ tsp. pepper, and remaining 3 Tbsp. vinegar and ½ tsp. salt. Season chicken and corn with salt and pepper to taste. Serve with coleslaw and reserved mayonnaise mixture.

time-saving tip: Dice leftover grilled chicken, and then combine with leftover slaw for a tasty lunch.

Shrimp and Grits

MAKES 6 SERVINGS
HANDS-ON TIME: 30 MIN.   **TOTAL TIME: 35 MIN.**

1½ lb. unpeeled, large raw shrimp (31/40 count)
1   lb. fresh asparagus
3   cups chicken broth
1   cup uncooked quick-cooking grits
½   cup half-and-half
4   Tbsp. butter, divided
1   (8-oz.) package sliced fresh mushrooms
1   bunch green onions, cut into ½-inch pieces
½   tsp. dried thyme
½   tsp. salt
Garnish: fresh thyme sprigs

sidekick: **SIMPLE SPINACH SALAD** Gently toss fresh baby spinach leaves, and thinly sliced red onions with bottled balsamic vinaigrette.

1. Peel shrimp; devein, if desired. Snap off and discard tough ends of asparagus. Cut asparagus into 1-inch pieces.

2. Bring chicken broth to a boil in a medium saucepan over medium-high heat; whisk in grits and half-and-half. Cook, whisking constantly, 7 minutes or until thickened. Remove from heat. Stir in 2 Tbsp. butter. Keep warm.

3. Melt remaining 2 Tbsp. butter in a large skillet over medium-high heat. Add asparagus, mushrooms, green onions, and thyme, and sauté 3 to 4 minutes. Add shrimp, and cook 2 to 3 minutes. Stir in salt; cook 3 minutes or just until shrimp turn pink. Serve immediately over warm grits. Garnish, if desired.

Roasted Tomato-and-Feta Shrimp

MAKES 6 SERVINGS
HANDS-ON TIME: 10 MIN.   **TOTAL TIME: 35 MIN.**

2	pt. grape tomatoes	½	cup chopped jarred roasted red bell peppers
3	garlic cloves, sliced	½	cup chopped fresh flat-leaf parsley
3	Tbsp. olive oil	1	(4-oz.) package crumbled feta cheese
1	tsp. kosher salt	2	Tbsp. fresh lemon juice
½	tsp. pepper		Crusty French bread, sliced
1½	lb. peeled and deveined, medium-size raw shrimp (31/40 count)		

1. Preheat oven to 450°. Place tomatoes and next 4 ingredients in a 13- x 9-inch baking dish, tossing gently to coat. Bake 15 minutes. Stir in shrimp and peppers. Bake 10 to 15 minutes or just until shrimp turn pink. Toss with parsley, feta cheese, and lemon juice. Serve immediately with crusty French bread.

flavor profile: shrimp

Fresh uncooked shrimp is very perishable, so use it within 2 days of purchase. After bringing it home, rinse thoroughly under cold running water, and pat dry with paper towels. Cover shrimp loosely with wax paper so that air can circulate around it; store in the coolest part of the refrigerator, preferably on a bed of ice. Shrimp can be frozen, but they lose some of their texture after thawing.

for company

Spicy Shrimp Noodle Bowl

MAKES 4 SERVINGS
HANDS-ON TIME: 15 MIN.   **TOTAL TIME: 20 MIN.**

1	(8.2-oz.) package soy-ginger-flavored Asian-style noodles	1	cup fresh snow peas, trimmed and cut into 1-inch pieces
2	(14.5-oz.) cans chicken broth		
1	lb. peeled and deveined, medium-size raw shrimp (31/40 count)	¾	cup matchstick carrots
		¼	cup loosely packed fresh cilantro leaves
¼	cup spicy Szechuan sauce	3	green onions, thinly sliced
2	cups shredded napa cabbage		

1. Cook noodles according to package directions, omitting flavor packet; drain.

2. Stir together flavor packet from noodles and chicken broth in a 3-qt. saucepan. Bring to a boil; add shrimp, and cook 3 minutes. Stir in Szechuan sauce and next 3 ingredients. Cook 2 minutes. Stir in noodles, cilantro, and green onions.

Note: We tested with Annie Chun's All Natural Asian Cuisine Soy Ginger Meal Starter and House of Tsang Szechuan Spicy Stir Fry Sauce.

savvy secret
from Vanessa:

Choose shrimp that are firm in texture, and avoid any that have dark spots. Add additional fresh cilantro and a squeeze of lime juice for extra flavor.

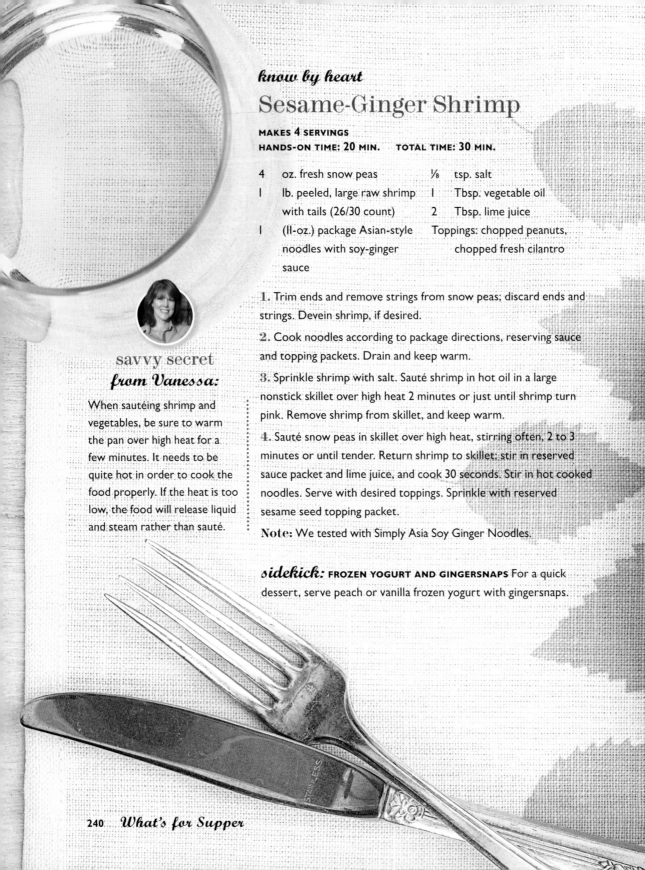

know by heart
Sesame-Ginger Shrimp

MAKES 4 SERVINGS
HANDS-ON TIME: 20 MIN.   **TOTAL TIME: 30 MIN.**

4	oz. fresh snow peas	⅛	tsp. salt
1	lb. peeled, large raw shrimp with tails (26/30 count)	1	Tbsp. vegetable oil
1	(11-oz.) package Asian-style noodles with soy-ginger sauce	2	Tbsp. lime juice
			Toppings: chopped peanuts, chopped fresh cilantro

1. Trim ends and remove strings from snow peas; discard ends and strings. Devein shrimp, if desired.

2. Cook noodles according to package directions, reserving sauce and topping packets. Drain and keep warm.

3. Sprinkle shrimp with salt. Sauté shrimp in hot oil in a large nonstick skillet over high heat 2 minutes or just until shrimp turn pink. Remove shrimp from skillet, and keep warm.

4. Sauté snow peas in skillet over high heat, stirring often, 2 to 3 minutes or until tender. Return shrimp to skillet; stir in reserved sauce packet and lime juice, and cook 30 seconds. Stir in hot cooked noodles. Serve with desired toppings. Sprinkle with reserved sesame seed topping packet.

Note: We tested with Simply Asia Soy Ginger Noodles.

sidekick: **FROZEN YOGURT AND GINGERSNAPS** For a quick dessert, serve peach or vanilla frozen yogurt with gingersnaps.

savvy secret
from Vanessa:

When sautéing shrimp and vegetables, be sure to warm the pan over high heat for a few minutes. It needs to be quite hot in order to cook the food properly. If the heat is too low, the food will release liquid and steam rather than sauté.

for company

Pickled Okra and Shrimp Salad

MAKES 6 SERVINGS
HANDS-ON TIME: 10 MIN.   TOTAL TIME: 40 MIN.

1	(3-oz.) package boil-in-bag shrimp-and-crab boil	⅓	cup mayonnaise
1½	lb. peeled and deveined, medium-size raw shrimp (31/40 count)	3	Tbsp. minced red onion
		½	tsp. lime zest
		3	Tbsp. fresh lime juice
½	cup sliced sweet-hot pickled okra	¼	tsp. pepper
		⅛	tsp. salt
1	(4-oz.) jar diced pimiento, drained	3	large avocados, sliced
		Garnish: lime zest	

table talk: Invite a group of friends over for a salad night and ask each friend to bring his or her favorite salad. Encourage them to bring a dish that evokes a memory. Ask friends to bring extra copies of the recipe to share with the group.

1. Bring 8 cups water to a boil in a 3-qt. saucepan; add crab boil, and cook 5 minutes. Add shrimp; cover, remove from heat, and let stand 10 minutes or just until shrimp turn pink. Drain and cool 10 minutes.

2. Meanwhile, combine pickled okra and next 7 ingredients. Add shrimp, and serve immediately over avocado slices, or cover and chill until ready to serve. Garnish, if desired.

sidekick: **TOASTED CHEESE BAGUETTES** Spread a thin layer of softened butter onto 1 side of 12 (½-inch-thick) French bread baguette slices. Bake at 425° for 4 minutes or until toasted. Combine 2 Tbsp. mayonnaise with 1 cup grated extra-sharp Cheddar cheese. Spread onto 1 side of bread. Bake 5 to 6 minutes or until cheese is melted.

kid favorite

Barbecue Shrimp

MAKES 6 SERVINGS
HANDS-ON TIME: 10 MIN.   **TOTAL TIME: 35 MIN.**

1½ lb. unpeeled jumbo raw
     shrimp (21/25 count)
1   large lemon, cut into wedges
1   (0.7-oz.) envelope Italian
     dressing mix

½   cup butter, melted
½   cup chopped fresh
     flat-leaf parsley

1. Preheat oven to 425°. Place shrimp and lemon in a 13- x 9-inch baking dish. Stir together dressing mix and butter. Pour butter mixture over shrimp, stirring to coat.

2. Bake at 425° for 20 to 25 minutes or just until shrimp turn pink.

3. Remove shrimp mixture from oven, and sprinkle with parsley.

sidekick: **TEXAS TOAST** While the shrimp are baking to perfection, you can add some frozen Texas toast to the oven. Bake 6 slices according to package directions, and use the bread to sop up the rich buttery sauce.

savvy secret
from Vanessa:

If purchasing shrimp with shells, make sure the shells are tightly intact. Fresh seafood is best stored packed in ice.

Shrimp Destin

MAKES 4 SERVINGS
HANDS-ON TIME: 30 MIN.   TOTAL TIME: 32 MIN.

2	lb. unpeeled, large raw shrimp (26/30 count)	⅛	tsp. salt
½	cup butter	1	Tbsp. chopped fresh dill or 1 tsp. dried dillweed
⅓	cup chopped green onions	1	Tbsp. chopped fresh parsley
1	Tbsp. minced garlic	4	(1.3-oz.) French rolls, split and toasted
¼	cup dry white wine		
1	tsp. lemon juice		Garnishes: fresh dill, sliced green onions
¼	tsp. freshly ground pepper		

1. Peel shrimp, leaving tails on, if desired; devein shrimp, if desired.

2. Melt butter in a large skillet over medium heat; add green onions and garlic, and sauté 2 minutes or until tender. Add shrimp, wine, and next 3 ingredients. Cook over medium heat, stirring occasionally, 5 minutes or just until shrimp turn pink. Remove from heat; stir in chopped dill and parsley.

3. Place toasted roll halves on 4 individual serving plates. Spoon shrimp mixture over toasted rolls, and garnish, if desired. Serve immediately.

sidekick: **CINNAMON PINEAPPLE:** Drain 2 (20-oz.) cans pineapple chunks in juice, reserving ¼ cup juice. Melt 1 Tbsp. butter in a large nonstick skillet over medium heat; add pineapple chunks, reserved juice, 2 Tbsp. brown sugar, 1 Tbsp. rum, and ½ tsp. ground cinnamon. Bring to a boil; reduce heat to low, and simmer, stirring frequently, 5 minutes.

time-saving tip:

Purchase 1½ lb. already peeled and deveined raw shrimp, and you're ready to start cooking.

Salmon with Parmesan-Herb Crust

MAKES 4 SERVINGS
HANDS-ON TIME: 15 MIN.   **TOTAL TIME: 35 MIN.**

4	(6-oz.) salmon fillets
¼	tsp. salt
1	Tbsp. fresh lime juice
1	tsp. olive oil
½	cup fine, dry breadcrumbs
½	cup (2 oz.) shredded Parmesan cheese
2	Tbsp. melted butter
1½	tsp. salt-free tomato-basil seasoning blend
	Lime wedges

1. Preheat oven to 375°. Sprinkle salmon with salt.

2. Place salmon on a lightly greased aluminum foil-lined 15- x 10-inch jelly-roll pan; pour lime juice and olive oil over salmon.

3. Stir together breadcrumbs and next 3 ingredients; spread mixture over salmon.

4. Bake at 375° for 20 minutes or just to desired degree of doneness. Serve immediately with lime wedges.

sidekick: **MASHED POTATOES** Boil 2 lb. peeled and chopped potatoes until tender; drain and mash. Stir in 1 cup warm milk, 3 oz. softened cream cheese, 1 Tbsp. chopped fresh chives, ½ tsp. salt, and ¼ tsp. pepper. Serve immediately.

flavor profile: Parmesan cheese

Perhaps the most widely used hard cheese, it's made from skim cow's milk and has a straw color. Parmigiano-Reggiano cheese is considered the finest of Parmesan. It has an appealing grainy texture and a rich and strong nutty flavor. This grade of Parmesan must be aged at least 12 months and is specific to the Italian province bearing its name—Parma. Its piquant quality makes it a versatile cheese that can be grated and incorporated into soups, salads, and pasta dishes.

Grilled Grouper with Watermelon Salsa

MAKES 4 SERVINGS
HANDS-ON TIME: 21 MIN.   TOTAL TIME: 21 MIN.

4   (4-oz.) grouper fillets
1   tsp. freshly ground pepper
1   tsp. salt, divided
3   Tbsp. olive oil, divided
2   cups chopped seedless watermelon
¼   cup chopped pitted kalamata olives
½   English cucumber, chopped
1   small jalapeño pepper, seeded and minced
2   Tbsp. minced red onion
2   Tbsp. white balsamic vinegar

1. Preheat grill to 350° to 400° (medium-high) heat. Sprinkle grouper with pepper and ½ tsp. salt. Drizzle with 2 Tbsp. olive oil.

2. Grill fish, covered with grill lid, 3 to 4 minutes on each side or just until fish begins to flake when poked with the tip of a sharp knife and is opaque in center.

3. Combine chopped watermelon, next 5 ingredients, and remaining ½ tsp. salt and 1 Tbsp. olive oil. Serve with grilled fish.

flavor profile: watermelon

Watermelon has surprising versatility. Aside from its traditional uses as a refreshing snack or dessert, it fits nicely into recipes for salsas, relishes, salads, and beverages. Choose firm, symmetrical, unblemished melons without cracks or soft spots. When buying precut watermelon, look for deep color, dark seeds with flesh firmly attached to seeds (unless it's seedless), and a sweet, fruity fragrance.

savvy secret
from Vanessa:

Fresh crabmeat is the key to creating a great crab cake, but using a crunchy coating and pan-frying them is the way to make a deliciously crisp version.

for company
Crunchy Crab Cakes

MAKES 4 SERVINGS
HANDS-ON TIME: 23 MIN.   **TOTAL TIME: 25 MIN.**

1	(16-oz.) package fresh lump crabmeat, drained	2	Tbsp. mayonnaise
2	tsp. lemon zest	1	tsp. Old Bay seasoning
2	Tbsp. lemon juice	2	tsp. Dijon mustard
1	(4-oz.) jar diced pimiento, well drained	1	cup panko (Japanese breadcrumbs), divided
2	green onions, chopped	¼	cup canola oil
1	large egg, lightly beaten		Lemon wedges

1. Pick crabmeat, removing any bits of shell.

2. Stir together lemon zest, and next 7 ingredients until well blended. Gently fold in crabmeat and ½ cup breadcrumbs.

3. Shape mixture into 8 patties. Dredge patties in remaining ½ cup breadcrumbs.

4. Cook half of patties in 2 Tbsp. hot oil in a large nonstick skillet over medium heat 2 minutes on each side or until golden brown; drain on a wire rack. Repeat procedure with remaining oil and patties.

5. Serve crab cakes with lemon wedges.

sidekick: **ARUGULA-GRAPE TOMATO SALAD** Toss together 1 (5-oz.) package arugula; 1 pt. grape tomatoes, halved; 2 Tbsp. fresh lemon juice; 2 Tbsp. olive oil; and ½ tsp. salt. Serve immediately.

for company

Steamed Mussels with Herbs

MAKES 4 SERVINGS
HANDS-ON TIME: 23 MIN.   **TOTAL TIME: 23 MIN.**

2	lb. fresh mussels	2	Tbsp. Dijon mustard
4	garlic cloves, minced	1	(14.5-oz.) can vegetable broth
2	shallots, minced	¼	tsp. salt
2	Tbsp. olive oil	¼	cup chopped fresh basil
2	cups dry white wine	¼	cup chopped fresh cilantro

1. Scrub mussels thoroughly with a scrub brush, removing beards. Discard any opened shells.

2. Sauté garlic and shallots in hot oil in a Dutch oven over medium heat 1 to 2 minutes. Stir in wine and mustard; cook 2 to 3 minutes. Add broth and salt, and bring to a boil. Add mussels. Cook, covered, stirring occasionally, 5 minutes or until all mussels have opened. Remove from heat. Stir in basil and cilantro.

sidekick: **BACON-BLUE CHEESE SALAD** Combine 3 cups torn frisée leaves, 2 cups diagonally cut Belgian endive, and ½ cup thinly sliced radicchio. Cook 2 slices bacon in a large nonstick skillet over medium heat until crisp. Remove bacon from pan, and drain on paper towels, reserving drippings in skillet; crumble bacon. Sauté ⅛ cup chopped shallots in hot drippings 30 seconds. Remove from heat; stir in 1 Tbsp. Champagne vinegar, 2 tsp. maple syrup, ½ tsp. Dijon mustard, ⅛ tsp. salt, and a dash of freshly ground pepper. Whisk in ½ tsp. olive oil. Pour dressing over salad greens; toss well to combine. Add crumbled bacon and ½ cup blue cheese to greens; toss gently.

metric equivalents

The recipes that appear in this cookbook use the standard U.S. method for measuring liquid and dry or solid ingredients (teaspoons, tablespoons, and cups). The information on this chart is provided to help cooks outside the United States successfully use these recipes. All equivalents are approximate.

Metric Equivalents for Different Types of Ingredients

A standard cup measure of a dry or solid ingredient will vary in weight depending on the type of ingredient. A standard cup of liquid is the same volume for any type of liquid. Use the following chart when converting standard cup measures to grams (weight) or milliliters (volume).

Standard Cup	Fine Powder (ex. flour)	Grain (ex. rice)	Granular (ex. sugar)	Liquid Solids (ex. butter)	Liquid (ex. milk)
1	140 g	150 g	190 g	200 g	240 ml
3/4	105 g	113 g	143 g	150 g	180 ml
2/3	93 g	100 g	125 g	133 g	160 ml
1/2	70 g	75 g	95 g	100 g	120 ml
1/3	47 g	50 g	63 g	67 g	80 ml
1/4	35 g	38 g	48 g	50 g	60 ml
1/8	18 g	19 g	24 g	25 g	30 ml

Useful Equivalents for Liquid Ingredients by Volume

1/4 tsp						=	1 ml	
1/2 tsp						=	2 ml	
1 tsp						=	5 ml	
3 tsp	=	1 Tbsp			=	1/2 fl oz	=	15 ml
		2 Tbsp	=	1/8 cup	=	1 fl oz	=	30 ml
		4 Tbsp	=	1/4 cup	=	2 fl oz	=	60 ml
		5 1/3 Tbsp	=	1/3 cup	=	3 fl oz	=	80 ml
		8 Tbsp	=	1/2 cup	=	4 fl oz	=	120 ml
		10 2/3 Tbsp	=	2/3 cup	=	5 fl oz	=	160 ml
		12 Tbsp	=	3/4 cup	=	6 fl oz	=	180 ml
		16 Tbsp	=	1 cup	=	8 fl oz	=	240 ml
		1 pt	=	2 cups	=	16 fl oz	=	480 ml
		1 qt	=	4 cups	=	32 fl oz	=	960 ml
						33 fl oz	=	1000 ml = 1 l

Useful Equivalents for Dry Ingredients by Weight

(To convert ounces to grams, multiply the number of ounces by 30.)

1 oz	=	1/16 lb	=	30 g
4 oz	=	1/4 lb	=	120 g
8 oz	=	1/2 lb	=	240 g
12 oz	=	3/4 lb	=	360 g
16 oz	=	1 lb	=	480 g

Useful Equivalents for Length

(To convert inches to centimeters, multiply the number of inches by 2.5.)

1 in					=	2.5 cm	
6 in	=	1/2 ft			=	15 cm	
12 in	=	1 ft			=	30 cm	
36 in	=	3 ft	=	1 yd	=	90 cm	
40 in					=	100 cm	= 1 m

Useful Equivalents for Cooking/Oven Temperatures

	Fahrenheit	Celsius	Gas Mark
Freeze water	32° F	0° C	
Room temperature	68° F	20° C	
Boil water	212° F	100° C	
Bake	325° F	160° C	3
	350° F	180° C	4
	375° F	190° C	5
	400° F	200° C	6
	425° F	220° C	7
	450° F	230° C	8
Broil			Grill

index